Renate Bruce-Weber

Die fröhliche
VIOLINE

Band 2

Ausbau der 1. Lage und
Einführung in die 3. Lage

ED 7786

SCHOTT

Mainz · London · Madrid · New York · Paris · Tokyo · Toronto

Inhalt

Impressum:
Bestellnummer ED 7786
ISMN M-001-08087-3
© 1991 Schott Musik International, Mainz
Printed in Germany · BSS 47025

Vorwort

Der zweite Band der „Fröhlichen Violine" führt die zweite und dritte Griffart ein (in der zweiten Griffart liegt der Halbton zwischen dem 3. und 4. Finger, in der dritten Griffart zwischen dem 1. und 2. Finger). Außerdem enthält er eine ausführliche Einführung in die dritte Lage unter ausschließlicher Verwendung der zweiten Griffart und ein Kapitel zur Verbindung der ersten und dritten Lage.

Bogentechnisch liegen die Schwerpunkte weiterhin auf den „Grundstricharten". Zur gezielten Übung bestimmter Bogenstriche befindet sich am Ende des Bandes eine schwerpunktmäßige Zusammenstellung der verschiedenen Stricharten.

Wie im ersten Band der „Fröhlichen Violine" habe ich versucht, technische Schwierigkeiten in Lieder und Stücke zu „verpacken", die den Schüler ansprechen und ihm Spaß machen. Darüber hinaus bietet dieser Band gezielte Kompositions- und Improvisationsaufgaben an, die den Schüler zu eigener Kreativität anregen sollen.

Ich danke Xaver Poncette für seine zweiten Stimmen, Wilhelm Isselmann für seine Anregungen in bezug auf Spielmaterial in der dritten Lage und besonders Mark für seine engagierte Mitarbeit an dieser Schule.

Renate Bruce-Weber

— Marilis neue Geige —

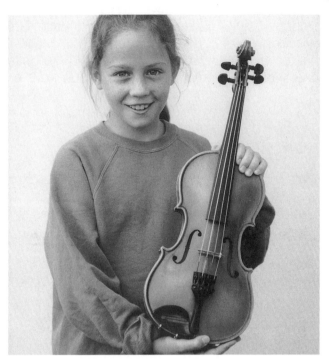

"Schau her!" sagt Marili. "Ich habe eine neue Geige." Marili ist sehr stolz. Sie spielt ein wenig darauf und betrachtet sie von allen Seiten. Da erblickt sie in der Geige einen Zettel mit der Aufschrift „Stradivari".

Stradivari? War das nicht einer der berühmtesten Geigenbauer?
Was meinst du, ob Marili da wirklich eine echte Stradivarigeige in den Händen hält?

Nein, natürlich nicht! Viele Geigenfabriken kleben heute Zettel mit Stradivaris Namen in die Schülergeigen, weil sie nach einem Stradivarimodell gefertigt sind, oder auch nur aus Werbezwecken.
Aber wer war denn nun eigentlich dieser „Stradivari"?

Antonio Stradivari

Antonio Stradivari lebte von 1644–1737 in der berühmten italienischen Geigenbauerstadt Cremona und hat in
seinem langen Leben über 1000 Instrumente, Geigen,
aber auch Bratschen und Celli gebaut. Die Musiker und
Sammler schwärmten zu allen Zeiten von seinen Instru-
menten. So lesen wir in einem alten Geigenfachbuch:
„Der göttliche Stradivari. Er war ein Zauberer... der
größte, den Cremona hervorgebracht hat. Mit dem un-
fehlbaren Scharfblick, der das Genie auszeichnet, er-
kannte er die unfaßbaren Beziehungen zwischen dem
schwingenden Holz und dem schmalen Kästchen, in
dem diese Schwingungen zu Tönen werden. Viele Ge-
heimnisse waren ihm bekannt, geheimes Wissen um das
Leben des Holzes und der Lacke, deren Zusammenset-
zung uns bis heute ein unlösbares Rätsel ist."

Noch heute spielen viele berühmte Geiger auf den wun-
dervollen Geigen von Antonio Stradivari, und auch die
bisher teuerste Violine hat er gebaut. Sie wurde 1988
von einem Londoner Auktionshaus für rund 1,5 Millionen
Mark verkauft.

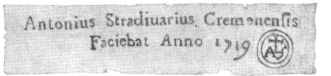

Stradivaris Geigenzettel

Antonio Stradivari
Kupferstich von A. Morilleron

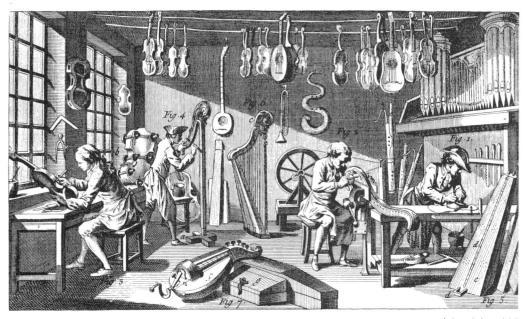

Instrumentenbauwerkstatt
Kupferstich aus dem 17. Jahrhundert

Die
zweite Griffart

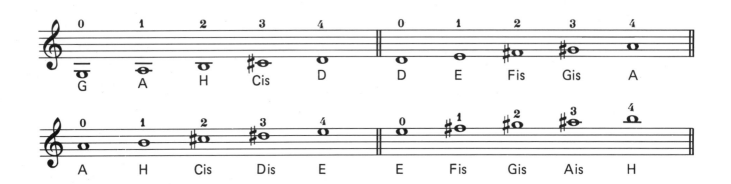

Die Schlangen klappern wieder

R. B-W.

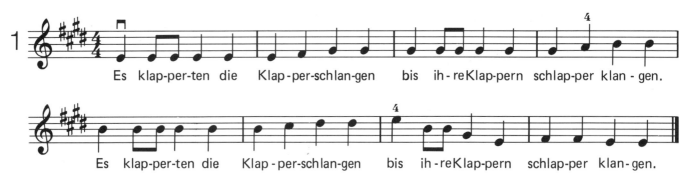

Es klap-per-ten die Klap-per-schlan-gen bis ih-re Klap-pern schlap-per klan-gen.

Es klap-per-ten die Klap-per-schlan-gen bis ih-re Klap-pern schlap-per klan-gen.

Die E-Dur-Tonleiter

2 a

b

Der Dackelgeburtstag

R. B-W.

3

Im Hau - se Nummer Sech-zehn a, da fei - ert heut' die E - ri - ka just

ei - nen ganz be - sond'-ren Tag, mit D fängt's an, wer ra - ten mag.

2. An diesem Tage ist das Körbchen
bunt verziert mit kleinen Herzchen,
und Geschenke gibt es auch,
wie es bei uns ist der Brauch.

3. Da liegen fein sortiert beim Körbchen
zwei, drei Knochen und ein Würstchen,
eine Schleife fürs Halsband,
Pantoffeln gar aus rotem Samt.

4. Und statt der Torte gibt's Filet
und Hühnerleber in Gelee
und eine Wand'rung ohne Ziel,
am Schluß noch ein Geländespiel.

5. Jetzt laß ich euch nicht länger warten.
Sicher habt ihr's schon erraten:
das Geburtstagskind der Stund'
heißt Purzel, unser Dackelhund.

Die A-Dur-Tonleiter

4 a

b

Die Striche unter den Achtelnoten zeigen an, daß diese sehr breit und dicht aneinander gespielt werden sollen. Diesen Bogenstrich in der Mitte des Bogens nennt man Detaché. Erinnerst du dich, was die Punkte unter den Viertelnoten bedeuten? Richtig, sie zeigen an, daß die Noten kurz und mit einer deutlichen Pause gespielt werden sollen. Der Strich ist ein schneller, gut auf der Saite liegender Strich, und man nennt ihn Martelé.

Auf dem Wasser zu singen

Kanon aus England

5

Row,   row,   row the boat,   gent - ly down the   stream.____
Sacht,   sacht,   ru - dern wir,   Wel - len gibt es   kaum.____

Mer - ri - ly, mer - ri - ly,   mer - ri - ly, mer - ri - ly, life   is   but   a   dream.____
Schwe - re - los, mü - he - los   glei - tet heut' un - ser Floß, es   ist   wie   ein   Traum.____

Deutscher Text: Renate Bruce-Weber

Die H-Dur-Tonleiter

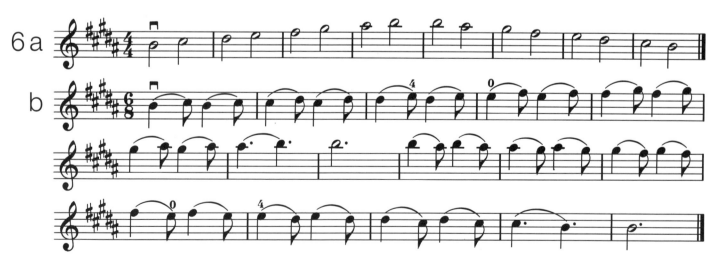

6 a

b

Wir transponieren wieder

7 Purzel rettet eine Maus

R. B-W.

Fing die Kat - ze ei - ne Maus, kam der Pur - zel g'rad nach Haus, kläfft die
Kat - ze wü - tend an, daß die Maus ent - wi - schen kann.

© B. Schott's Söhne, Mainz, 1991

Dieses Lied wollen wir wie das Mäuschen- und das Regenlied (Nr. 91 und Nr. 92 im ersten Band der „Fröhlichen Violine") **transponieren**. Kannst du dich noch an die Klettertonleiter (Band 1, Nr. 84) erinnern? Versuche, ob du sie noch spielen kannst, und paß dabei auf, wo die Halbtöne liegen!

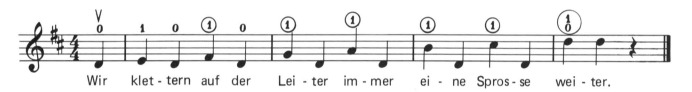

Wir klet - tern auf der Lei - ter im - mer ei - ne Spros - se wei - ter.

Wenn du unser Lied „Purzel rettet eine Maus" sicher, am besten auswendig, spielen kannst, spiele den Anfang der Klettertonleiter bis zum Fis und beginne dort mit dem Lied. Als nächstes kletterst du zum G und spielst das Lied von G aus. Dies läßt sich beliebig fortsetzen, das Lied klingt also immer höher.

Auf diese Weise kannst du auch die ersten drei Lieder und die Tonleitern aus diesem Band transponieren, und wenn es dir Spaß macht, sogar alle anderen Lieder in dieser Griffart, die mit dem ersten Finger beginnen. Sicherlich hast du schon von anderen Geigern gehört, daß sie manchmal „in den Lagen" spielen. Nun, du tust es hiermit auch. Wenn du den letzten Ton der Klettertonleiter als Anfangston wählst, spielst du sogar schon in der siebten Lage. Auf der Geige zählt man bis zur 12. Lage.

Transponiere das Lied „Purzel rettet eine Maus" auch auf den anderen Saiten. Schreibe zuerst die Klettertonleiter auf.

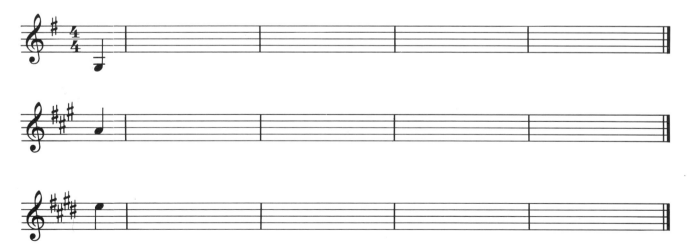

Drei alte Bekannte

Die alte Brücke

aus Rumänien

Die al - te Brük - ke steht nicht mehr dort, das Was-ser kam und

riß sie mit fort. Un - ten am Fluß 'ne neu - e wir bau'n,

und die wird stark und schö - ner aus - schau'n.

Deutscher Text: Renate Bruce-Weber

Die alte Brücke – etwas verändert

R. B-W.

Kleine Melodie

R. B-W.

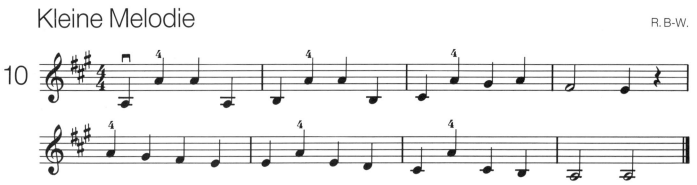

Hast du schon einmal ein Orchester gesehen und gehört? Wie heißt der Mann oder die Frau, die auf dem Podest vor den Musikern steht?

Richtig – Dirigent(in). Überlege dir, welche Aufgabe ein Dirigent hat!

Vielleicht magst du bei den Liedern Nr. 11 und Nr. 13 auch einmal Dirigent spielen? Schau dir zuerst an, in welcher Taktart das Lied steht. Die betonte Zählzeit des Taktes, die Eins, schlägt der Dirigent immer von oben nach unten. Die Figur des Dreiertaktes gleicht einem Dreieck. Die Hand geht nach unten, nach außen, schräg nach oben. Die Figur des Vierertaktes sieht so aus (die Hand geht nach unten, nach innen, nach außen und dann schräg nach oben):

Bevor der Dirigent anfängt, den Takt zu schlagen, muß er überlegen, in welchem Tempo er das Musikstück oder das Lied empfindet. Dann gibt er genau in diesem Tempo den Einsatz. Was tut er am Ende des Stückes, damit alle gemeinsam aufhören?

Der Dirigent überlegt sich auch, wie er die Musik gestalten möchte, ob das Stück laut oder leise gespielt werden soll und welche Vortragszeichen der Komponist angegeben hat. Am Ende von unserem „Dirigierlied" steht zum Beispiel ein **„ritardando"**. „Ritardando" ist italienisch und bedeutet „langsamer werden". Das Wort wird meistens abgekürzt mit „rit.".

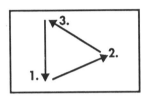
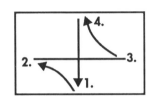

Dirigierlied

R. B-W.

Eins, zwei, drei, vier, di - ri - gie - ren kön-nen wir, oh-ne Stock und oh-ne Frack

wich - tig ist, es stimmt der Takt: eins und zwei und drei und vier und

eins und zwei und drei und vier und im - mer wei - ter drei und vier und

im - mer lau - ter drei und vier und eins, zwei, drei, vier di - ri - gie - ren kön - nen wir,

bis ich mei - ne Hand er - he - be und zum Schluß das Zei - chen ge - be.

Wir komponieren

Vielleicht hast du Lust, einmal ein eigenes Lied zu komponieren. Wie wär's mit „Alles, alles, alles kommt gerannt, -rannt, -rannt"? Als kleine Hilfe haben wir den Text schon als Liedtext gedruckt. Bevor du anfängst, sprich den Text sehr rhythmisch und überlege, welche Notenwerte du brauchst! Verwende die Noten der E-Dur-Tonleiter (siehe Nr. 2)! Wie müssen die Viertelnoten gespielt werden, damit sie zu dem Text passen, und wie schreibt man das?

Alles, alles, alles kommt gerannt, -rannt, -rannt

Komponist:

Al - les, al - les, al - les, kommt ge - rannt, - rannt, - rannt,

Hüh - ner, Zie - gen, E - sel, E - le - fant, - fant, - fant,

Hun - de, I - gel, Kin - der; al - le Hand in Hand,

denn da kommt der lust' - ge Mu - si - kant, - kant, - kant.

Verschiedene Meinungen

R. B-W.

Fritz sagt, wenn's reg - net, dann geh ich nicht raus. Franz sagt, wenn's reg - net, dann

bleib ich zu Haus. Nick sagt, wenn's reg - net, das macht kei - nen Spaß.

Max sagt, wenn's reg - net, dann werd ich ja naß! Nur der klei - ne A - dri - an

kann es nicht er - war - ten, nimmt den gro - ßen Re - gen-schirm, wa-tet in den Gar - ten.

2. Griffart

Baskisches Sommerlied

Satz: Mark Bruce

Träu - mend lieg ich auf der Wie - se, seh die Wol - ken ziehn.

Schick mit_ ih - nen mei - ne Grü - ße bis nach Bil - ba - o*) hin.

Wünscht', ich_ wär' ein Hir - te von zehn Scha - fen nur;

könn - te_ träu - men al - le Ta - ge in der_ grü - nen Flur.

© B. Schott's Söhne, Mainz, 1991

Deutscher Text: Renate Bruce-Weber

*) Bilbao liegt in Spanien und ist die Hauptstadt des Baskenlandes.

2. Griffart

Slowakisches Winterlied

Satz: Mark Bruce

Vög-lein im Win-ter, siehst trau-rig aus! Komm doch in mein klei-nes Fut-ter-haus!

Dort kannst dich la-ben an Korn und Sa-men, schüt-zen vor Käl-te und Win-des Braus.

Deutscher Text: Renate Bruce-Weber

Der schwungvolle Aufstrich

Die Viertelnote mit Punkt ♩ kennen wir schon. Bisher haben wir sie mit einem Martelé-Strich gespielt, bei dem der Bogen gut auf der Saite liegenbleiben mußte. Jetzt wollen wir sie mit einem schwungvollen Aufstrich spielen. Der Bogen darf dabei mit viel Geschwindigkeit von der Saite wegfliegen. Aber Achtung: Halte den Bogen gut in der Hand, damit du ihn bei der nächsten Note schön weich am Frosch wieder auf die Saite legen kannst.

Die kleine Note mit durchgestrichenem Fähnchen bezeichnet einen kurzen Vorschlag. Sie wird nicht als Achtelnote gespielt, sondern so kurz wie möglich vor der Hauptnote.

Hinkewalzer

R. B-W.

2. Griffart

In dem „Hinkewalzer" kommt wieder ein „ritardando" vor. Es steht in einem Überleitungstakt zum Anfangsthema. Merkst du, wie spannend die Musik wird, wenn du in dem Takt langsamer wirst? Das Thema spielst du dann wieder „a tempo", d. h. wieder im ursprünglichen Tempo.

Hast du Lust, dein eigenes Schwungstrichstück zu komponieren? Den Anfang haben wir schon aufgeschrieben.

Wie könnte es weitergehen?

Nasentanz zu Gimpelsbrunn (16. Jh.)

Spiele in diesem Stück die schwungvollen Aufstriche in der Mitte des Bogens!

Springtanz

R. B-W.
Satz: Mark Bruce

Wir rutschen nach oben

Im ersten Band der „Fröhlichen Violine" bist du schon mit deiner linken Hand in die Lagen geklettert. Dabei durfte der Finger von einer Lage in die andere springen, weil zwischendurch immer eine leere Saite vorkam. Wenn vor dem Lagenwechsel nun aber keine leere Saite steht, mußt du mit dem Finger rutschen und ihn dabei locker auf der Saite liegenlassen.

Der Oktavrutscher

Versuchen wir es zunächst mit einem großen Rutscher nach oben, dem Oktavrutscher. Spiele zuerst den hohen Ton in der ersten Lage, damit du ihn gut im Ohr hast. Das ist wichtig, denn wenn du dir den Zielton während des Rutschens vorstellst, findet der Finger ihn besser.

Dann versuche auch den Lagenwechsel nach unten. Achte darauf, daß auch dein **Handgelenk** und dein **Arm** wieder zurück in die erste Lage müssen.

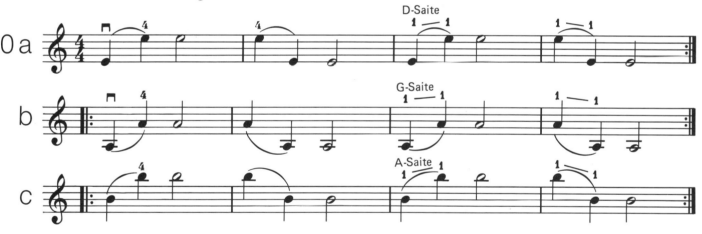

Rutsch-Tonleiter mit dem 1. Finger

Nun kannst du in der Ersten-Finger-Rutsch-Tonleiter auch kleinere Rutscher üben. Bitte spiele die Tonleiter vorher auch in der ersten Lage! Übe die Rutsch-Tonleiter auch auf den anderen Saiten!

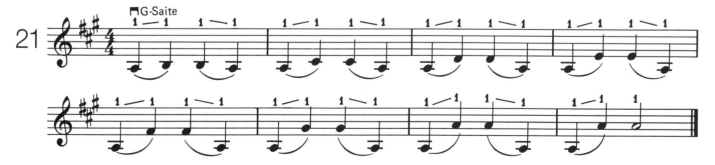

Barcarole

Mark Bruce

Barcarole. Zeichnung von Gérard Grandville

2. Griffart

Rondo

Rondo. Zeichnung von Gérard Grandville

aus einem alten Duettbuch um 1740

23

Das Rondo ist aus einem mittelalterlichen Tanzlied, dem „Rondeau", entstanden. Es war ein Rundgesang mit Chor und Solosänger, bei dem der Chor immer den gleichen „Refrain" sang, der Solist dagegen eine andere Melodie. Findest du in unserem Rondo den „Refrain", also den Teil, der sich wiederholt?

Wir verbinden die erste und zweite Griffart

Die A-Dur-Tonleiter durch zwei Oktaven

24

Wo sind in dieser Tonleiter die Halbtöne? Wo ist der dritte
Finger tief, und wo ist er hoch? In den folgenden Stücken
mußt du immer, bevor du anfängst zu spielen, überlegen:
Welche Vorzeichen hat das Stück? Was bedeutet das für
die Griffart?

Kleine Etüde in A-Dur

R. B-W.

25

Ich bin der frohe Hirtenknab'

aus Finnland
Satz: Mark Bruce

26
Ich bin der fro-he— Hir-ten-knab',mei-ne Her-de weid'ich auf und ab, ich

bin mit mei-nen Tie-ren froh und die Flö-te, die bläst so:

tu tu tu te li lu, tu tu tu te li lu.

Deutscher Text: Renate Bruce-Weber

Der 3. Finger in D-Dur

27

Spiele auswendig:

28
Ein Vo - gel woll - te Hoch - zeit ma - chen

Tim, der Pfeifer

aus Irland

29

Heu - te spielt der weit ge - rühm - te,__ ü - ber - all so sehr be - lieb - te__

und im Pfei - fen un - be - sieg - te Pfei - fer__ Tim aus__ Ir - land.

Spie - len kann er laut und leis', für den Jüng - ling, für den Greis.

Er be - kommt den er - sten Preis: Pfei - fer Tim aus Ir - land.

Deutscher Text: Renate Bruce-Weber

Wenn die Bettelleute tanzen

Satz: Mark Bruce

30

Wenn die Bet - tel - leu - te tan - zen, wak - keln Ko - ber und der Ran - zen.

Ei - a, ei - a, ei - a, so geht's, so geht's, so geht's;

ei, so geht's, so geht's, ei, so geht's, so geht's, wak - keln Ko - ber und der Ran - zen.

Ein Narrentanz (um 1340)

Rheinländer Narrentanz

Satz: Mark Bruce

31

Fine

D.C. al Fine

Gavotte

Christoph Willibald Gluck
1714–1787
Satz: Mark Bruce

Christoph Willibald Glucks Vater war Förster an einem Fürstenhof und er wollte, daß auch sein Sohn Förster wird. Doch dieser interessierte sich viel mehr für die Musik, und als er nicht Musiker werden durfte, riß er von zu Hause aus und verdiente sich als wandernder Musikant in Kirchen und Tanzsälen sein Brot. Nach einem Mathematikstudium fand er eine Stelle als Cellist in einer Privatkapelle in Mailand, wo er mit 27 Jahren seine erste Oper schrieb. Das war der Anfang einer großen Karriere als Opernkomponist. Unsere Gavotte stammt allerdings nicht aus einer seiner Opern, sondern aus dem Ballett „Don Juan".

Lithographie nach einem Gemälde von I. Duplessis

24

Spiegelkanon

Wolfgang Amadeus Mozart
1756–1791

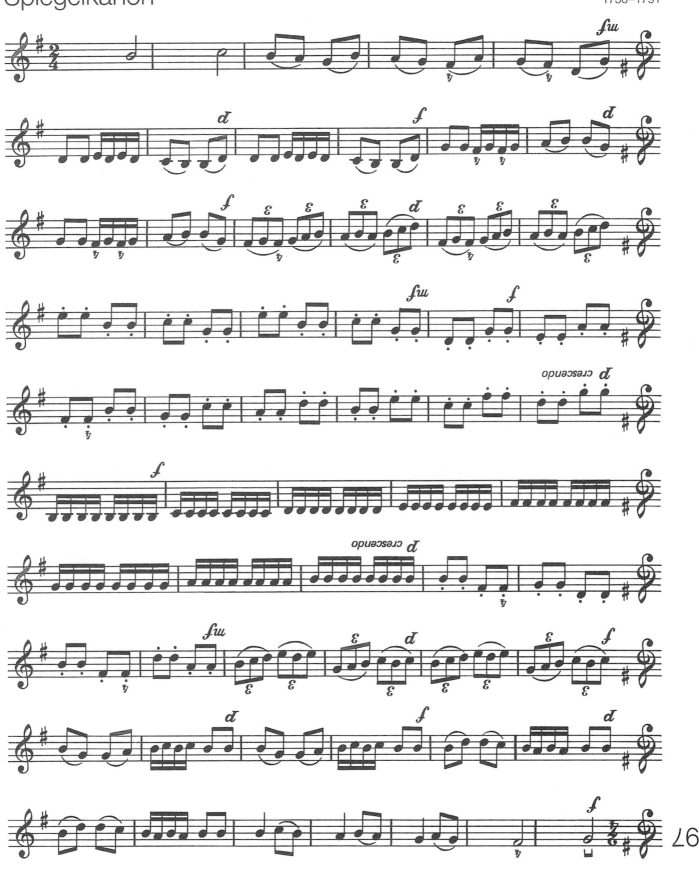

Spiegelkanon

Wolfgang Amadeus Mozart
1756–1791

1. + 3. Griffart

Deutscher Tanz

Wolfgang Amadeus Mozart
1756–1791
Satz: Mark Bruce

Fine

D.C. al Fine

Von dem großen Komponisten und berühmten Wunderkind **Wolfgang Amadeus Mozart** hast du sicherlich schon gehört. Er bekam mit vier Jahren Klavier- und mit sieben Jahren Geigenunterricht. Von Mozarts ganz außergewöhnlicher Begabung auch zum Geigenspiel erzählt die folgende Geschichte. Der Hoftrompeter Schachtner, ein Freund der Familie Mozart, berichtet, daß der Geiger Wenzl, Vater Leopold und Schachtner sich einmal zum Triospiel trafen:

„Wolfgangerl bat, daß er das 2te Violin spielen dürfte, der Papa aber verwies ihm seine närrische Bitte, weil er nicht die geringste Anweisung in dem Violin hatte, und Papa glaubte, daß er nicht das mindeste zu leisten im Stande wäre. Wolfgang sagte, um ein 2tes Violin zu spielen, braucht es ja wohl nicht, erst gelernt zu haben, und als Papa darauf bestand, daß er gleich fortgehen und uns nicht weiter beunruhigen sollte, fing Wolfgang an, bitterlich zu weinen, und trollte sich mit seinem Geigerl weg. Ich bat, daß man ihn möchte mit mir spielen lassen. Endlich sagte Papa, ‚Geig mit Herrn Schachtner, aber so still, daß man dich nicht hört. Sonst mußt du fort.‘ Das geschah… Bald merkte ich mit Erstaunen, daß ich da ganz überflüssig war. Ich legte still meine Geige weg, und sah ihren Herrn Papa an, dem bei dieser Szene die Tränen der Bewunderung… über die Wangen rollten, und so spielte er alle 6 Trios. Als wir fertig waren, wurde Wolfgang durch unsren Beifall so kühn, daß er behauptete, auch das erste Violin spielen zu können. Wir machten zum Spaße einen Versuch, und wir mußten uns fast zu Tode lachen, als er auch dies, wiewohl mit lauter unrechten und unregelmäßigen Applicaturen doch so spielte, daß er nie ganz stecken blieb.“

Die
dritte Griffart

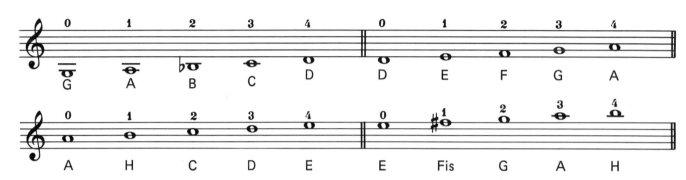

Der zweite Finger spielt auf der G-Saite in dieser Griffart ein „B". Vor der Note siehst du das Versetzungszeichen ♭, das die Note, vor der es steht, um einen halben Ton erniedrigt. So wird hier aus dem „H" ein „B".

An Regentagen zu singen

R. B-W.

34

"Heu - te ist ein schö - ner Tag!" ru - fen Sturm und Wind.
Auch der Wurm, der Re - gen mag, ist ganz froh ge - stimmt.

Frösch' und Krö - ten qua - ken laut, Schnek - ken ju - beln sehr.

Komm, wer sich ins Was - ser traut! Gum - mi - stie - fel her!

35 Das Mäuschen

R. B-W.

Was_ träumt wohl das_ Mäus - chen in __ sei - nem Mäu - se - bau?

Träumt von Käs' und Schin - ken und ei - ner Frau.

2. Was träumt wohl das Hündchen
in seinem Hundebett?
Träumt von Ball und Stöckchen
und Würsten fett.

3. Was träumt der kleine Geiger
in seinem Bettchen nur?
Träumt von schönen Klängen
in Moll und Dur.

36 Im Walde

aus Finnland
Satz: Mark Bruce

Tief im Wal - de fließt ein Bäch - lein, plätschernd dringt es an mein Ohr. Horch nur, wie es zart und lei - se singt dies klei - ne Lied mir vor. Horch nur, wie es zart und lei - se singt dies klei - ne Lied mir vor.

Deutscher Text: Renate Bruce-Weber

37 Alle Affen Alabamas

R. B-W.

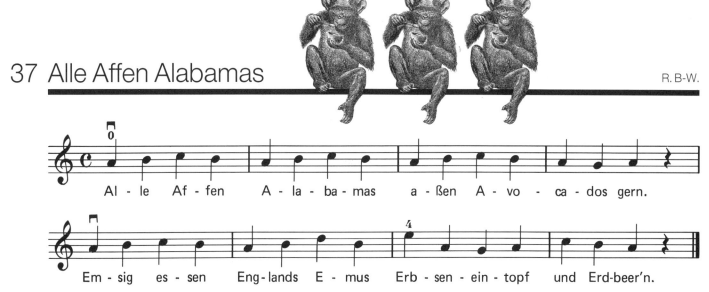

Al - le Af - fen A - la - ba - mas a - ßen A - vo - ca - dos gern.

Em - sig es - sen Eng - lands E - mus Erb - sen - ein - topf und Erd-beer'n.

Maienwind am Abend

Kanon aus Ungarn

38

Mai - en-wind am A-bend sacht läßt die Blät-ter we - hen, lieb-lich duf-tend in der Nacht

Flie - der - bäu - me ste - hen. Ap - fel - blü - ten dicht an dicht

schim - mern weiß im Mon - den - licht, weiß im Mon-den - licht.

Deutscher Text: Barbara Heuschober
Aus: F. Jöde/W. Träder, Alle singen, Bd. 2, B. Schott's Söhne, Mainz

Die Nachtigall

aus Rußland
Satz: Xaver Poncette

39

Lei - se sin - get die Nach - ti-gall ih - re Wei-se, in der Stil - le er -tönt es so rein;

klar, hell und fein schmei-chelt sich ein, lieb - li -cher Ton in der Däm-me-rung al-lein.

Mil - de und lind Sehn-sucht er-klingt, Nach - ti-gall singt von dem we-hen Her-zen mein.

Deutscher Text: Jutta Lehel
aus: Europäische Kinderlieder
hrsg. von Katalin Forrai, Schott, Mainz/Editio Musica, Budapest, 1967

3. Griffart

Moll-Dreiklänge

Englisches Seemannslied

Was ma-chen wir mit dem trunk'-nen See-mann? Was ma-chen wir mit dem trunk'-nen See-mann?

Was ma-chen wir mit dem trunk'-nen See - mann an dem frü - hen Mor - gen?

He ho, wie es schau-kelt! He ho, rauf und run - ter!

He ho, wie es schau-kelt an dem frü - hen Mor - gen.

Englischer Text:
What shall we do with the drunken sailor,
what shall we do with the drunken sailor,
what shall we do with the drunken sailor,
early in the morning.
Hooray and up she rises, hooray and up she rises,
Horray and up she rises, early in the morning.

Deutscher Text: Renate Bruce-Weber

> ist das Zeichen für einen „Akzent", eine Betonung.
Streiche den Anfang der halben Note ganz schnell!
Kannst du jetzt hören, wie das Schiff schaukelt?

In dem nächsten Stück wird eine Melodie, das „Thema", auf verschiedene Weise verändert. Kannst du beschreiben, wie die ersten zwei Variationen das Thema verändern? Was geschieht bei der dritten Variation? Schau sie dir genau an! Vergleiche besonders den Anfang und das Ende mit dem Thema! Na, findest du es heraus?

."sberK„ nam tnnen kinhcetsnoitisopmoK eseiD.
tleipseg sträwkcür amehT sad driw 3 noitairaV red nI

Thema und Variationen

R. B-W.

Wir komponieren

Hast du Lust, eine eigene Variation zu komponieren? Nimm als „Thema" das Lied „An Regentagen zu singen", oder denke dir aus den Tönen des Liedes ein eigenes Thema aus!

43

Spiele auswendig:

44

Frè - re Jac - ques, Frè - re Jac - ques,

He - jo, spann den Wa - gen an,

Heut' tan - zen wir wie Bel - la Bim - ba,

In welcher Tonart
stehen diese Lieder?

Wir spielen laut und leise

Die G-Dur-Tonleiter

Kannst du dich noch an die Zeichen *f* = forte und *p* = piano erinnern? Wie spielst du auf der Geige laut und leise? Probiere es aus: Spiele das Forte mit viel und das Piano mit wenig Bogen! Dann streiche das Forte näher am Steg und das Piano näher am Griffbrett! Was klingt am schönsten?

Echostück 1

R. B-W.
Satz: Xaver Poncette

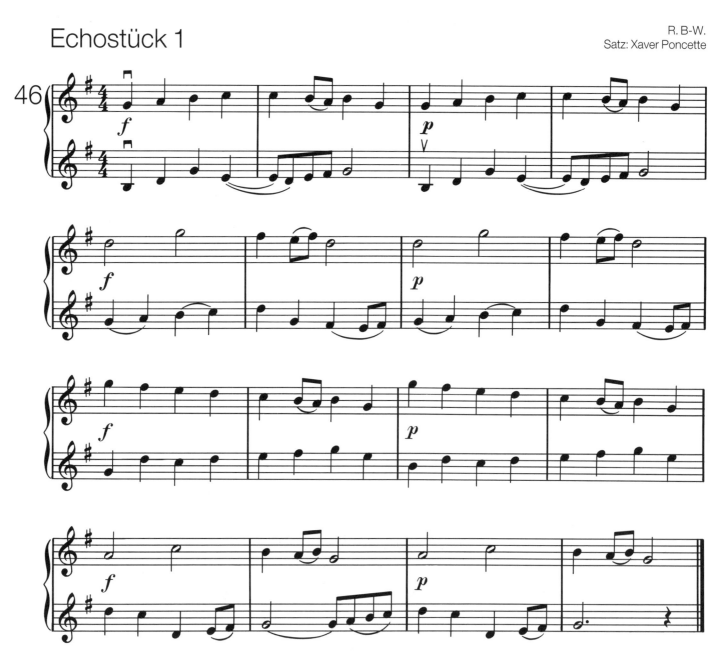

Sechzehntelnoten

Die C-Dur-Tonleiter

♪ = Sechzehntelnote ♫ = ♪♪ = ♪ ⌐ = Sechzehntelpause
Sechzehntelnoten sind doppelt so schnell wie Achtelnoten.

Die letzten Note von der „kleinen Eisenbahn" ist ein Flageolett. Wie bei dem Oktav-Flageolett, das du schon kennst, berührt man dabei die Saite nur ganz leicht. Spiele zum Üben zuerst den ganz normalen Schlußton C, nimm dann den Fingerdruck von der Saite und spiele mit dem Bogen in Stegnähe weiter! Welcher Ton erklingt jetzt? Es ist das G, das du sonst mit dem 2. Finger auf der E-Saite greifst. Aber der Flageoletton klingt ganz anders, nicht wahr? Er klingt ein bißchen wie der Pfiff einer Lokomotive.

Die kleine Eisenbahn

Mark Bruce

„Accelerando" ist das Gegenteil von „ritardando" und bedeutet: schneller werden.

Der C-Dur-Dreiklang

49

Erntelied

aus Dänemark
Satz: Xaver Poncette

50

Nun sind ge - mäht al - le Wie - sen und Fel - der, Heu und Korn sind ein-ge - fah -ren,
Äp - fel und Bir - nen sind auch schon ge - ern - tet, lu-stig geht's nun heim-wärts auf der

lie - gen gut ver - wahrt. Bin - det Korn zum Kranz, kommt zum Ern - te - tanz,
al - ler - letz- ten Fahrt.

Bur - schen, Mäd - chen, schnell her - bei, wir wol - len fröh - lich sein.

Deutscher Text: K. Haus/F. Möckl
aus: Lieder der Welt, B. Schott's Söhne, Mainz

Der G-Dur-Dreiklang

51

3. Griffart

Spiele auswendig:

52

Al - le Vö - gel sind schon da, Al - le Vö - gel

Als wir jüngst in Regensburg waren

aus Bayern
Satz: Xaver Poncette

53

Als wir jüngst in__ Re - gens-burg wa - ren, sind wir ü - ber den

Stru - del ge - fah - ren, da war'n vie - le Hol - den,

die mit - fah - ren woll - ten. Schwä - bi - sche, bay - ri - sche

Dirn - del, juch - hei -ras - sa, muß der Schiffs - mann fah - ren.

Marsch

aus einem alten Duettbuch um 1740

Wenn du das Wort „Marsch" hörst, weißt du, was das ist: Musik zum Marschieren, so wie ein „Tanz" Musik zum Tanzen ist. Da man aber langsamer und schneller gehen kann, gibt es auch verschiedene Arten von Märschen. Der langsamste ist der Trauermarsch. Auch ganz feierliche Märsche, wie z. B. der Einzug der Priester in Mozarts Oper „Die Zauberflöte", sind langsam. Du kennst sicher Militärmärsche. Auch sie sind verschieden schnell, in Deutschland 114 Schritte pro Minute, in Frankreich 140. Noch schneller ist der „Geschwindmarsch" (das berühmteste Beispiel dafür ist der "Radetzki-Marsch"). Außerdem gibt es noch Reitermärsche im 6/8-Takt.

Was für ein Marsch, denkt du, ist unser Marsch? Zu welcher Gelegenheit könnte man ihn spielen?

Bauerntanz

aus Mähren
Satz: Mark Bruce

Am Spinnrad

R. B-W.
Satz: Mark Bruce

56

Die böse 7

aus Kroatien
Satz: Mark Bruce

57

Trauriges Lied
Die Enttäuschung

aus England
Satz: Xaver Poncette

Noch eh der er - ste Son - nen - strahl, trieb's mich nach drau - ßen schon, im

schö - nen Mai - en mich zu er - freu - en am süs - sen Gei - gen - ton.

Deutscher Text: Renate Bruce-Weber

2. Kaum hatte ich ein Lied gespielt
ganz leise und ganz zart,
sah ich voll Wonnen
ein Mädchen kommen
von allerliebster Art.

3. Doch, ach, es hört mein Geigen nicht,
es läuft behend davon.
Ich seh die Sonn':
„Halt, Mädchen, komm!"
Ganz traurig wird mein Ton.

Fröhliches Lied
Im Schlaraffenland

Melodie: Renate Bruce-Weber
Text: Heinrich Hoffmann von Fallersleben

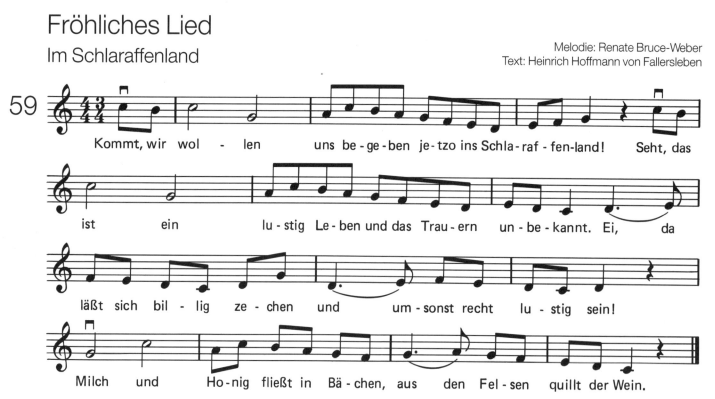

Kommt, wir wol - len uns be - ge - ben je - tzo ins Schla - raf - fen - land! Seht, das

ist ein lu - stig Le - ben und das Trau - ern un - be - kannt. Ei, da

läßt sich bil - lig ze - chen und um - sonst recht lu - stig sein!

Milch und Ho - nig fließt in Bä - chen, aus den Fel - sen quillt der Wein.

Doppelgriff-Training

Doppelgriffe in Moll

60

61

Trauriges Stück

Der einsame Dudelsackspieler

R. B-W.

62

Fröhliches Stück

Trompetenmenuett

Michel Corrette
1709–1795
Satz: Xaver Poncette

Fine

D.C. al Fine

Wir komponieren

Hast du Lust, ein *trauriges* Trompetenmenuett zu komponieren? Verwende dazu die vorgegebenen Töne und den Rhytmus aus den ersten acht Takten des „Trompetenmenuetts". Auf welchem Ton muß dein Stück enden?

Wir verbinden die erste und dritte Griffart

Bei den nächsten beiden Stücken mischen wir die dritte Griffart (Stolperstein 1) und die erste Griffart (Stolperstein 2). Spiele beide Stücke erst langsam und dann immer schneller und achte besonders auf den 2. Finger!

Wie wär's, wenn du in den nächsten Wochen zum Einspielen beim Üben mit den beiden Stolpersteinen beginnst? Du kannst die Reihenfolge auch vertauschen, also zuerst Stolperstein 2 und dann Stolperstein 1 spielen.

Marili spielt sich jeden Tag mit den „Stolpersteinen" ein.

Stolperstein 1

Erst langsam, dann schnell

65

Stolperstein 2

66

Spiele die Stolpersteine auch auf den anderen Saiten!

Die erste Chromatik

Eine Durtonleiter besteht, wie du weißt, aus Ganz- und Halbtonschritten. Es gibt auch eine Tonleiter, die nur aus Halbtonschritten (12 an der Zahl) besteht: das ist die *chromatische* Tonleiter. Ein kleiner Ausschnitt daraus befindet sich in dem folgenden Walzer und in dem „Cowboysong". Findest du diese chromatischen Stellen schon vor dem Spielen?

Kleiner chromatischer Walzer

R. B-W.

67

Deutscher Text: Renate Bruce-Weber

Cowboysong

aus Amerika

68

Hab ge - rit - ten mein Pferd all mein Leb - tag und Nacht. Hab die Rin - der ge-

trie - ben und den Colt gut be - wacht. Man kennt mich in Te - xas und

in I - da - ho: bin der gro - ße, der wil - de und der mu - ti - ge Cow - boy Joe.

Dur und Moll

Dur oder Moll?

In den folgenden Stücken mußt du überlegen, wo der zweite Finger tief und wo er hoch greift. Spiele den Unterschied sehr deutlich. Der Aufbau der Molltonleiter wird erst später erklärt (siehe S. 91). Sicher kannst du aber schon hören, daß Moll ganz anders klingt als Dur. Worin besteht der Unterschied?

R. B-W.

Diese Lieder stehen in Moll. Kannst du sie in Dur spielen?
Welcher Ton verändert sich?

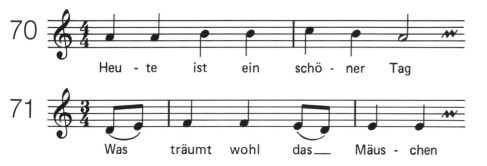

Diese Lieder stehen in Dur. Spiele sie in Moll.

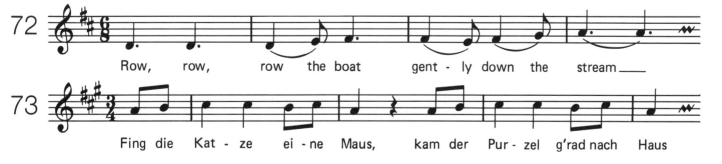

Russisches Schlaflied

Satz: Mark Bruce

Du mei - ne klei - ne mü - de Al - jo - scha,

hör un - ser Lied, dann schläfst du im Nu! Ganz lei - se sin - gen wir,

wie - gen das Bett - chen dir. Kol - ja spielt Ba - la - lai - ka da - zu.

Deutscher Text: Renate Bruce-Weber

Steht dieses Lied in Dur oder in Moll?

G-Dur-Tonleiter durch zwei Oktaven

Italienisches Frühlingslied

Satz: Mark Bruce

Deutscher Text: Renate Bruce-Weber

Musette

Johann Sebastian Bach
1685–1750
(aus der Englischen Suite Nr. 3)

Überlege dir die Dynamik (d. h. wo du laut und leise spielst) selber.

Musiker der Bach-Zeit
Stich aus dem 17. Jh.

Der 2. Finger in D-Dur

8a

b

Zum Reigen herbei

Melodie: Ernst Richter (1805–1876)
Text: Heinrich Hoffmann von Fallersleben (1798–1874)
Satz: Mark Bruce

79

Zum Rei - gen her - bei im fröh - li - chen Mai! Mit

Blü - ten und Zwei - gen be - kränzt euch zum Rei - gen! Im

fröh - li - chen Mai zum Rei - gen her - bei!

Georg Friedrich Händel

Im Jahre 1685 (in demselben Jahr wie Johann Sebastian Bach) wurde in Halle Georg Friedrich Händel geboren. Sein Vater war Barbier und Arzt, und wie so viele Väter wollte auch er lieber, daß sein Sohn einen „anständigen" Beruf erlernte, statt Musiker zu werden. Georg Friedrich schrieb sich also an der Universität ein, um Jura zu studieren, verließ dann aber schon ein Jahr später seine Geburtsstadt und wurde zweiter Geiger im Hamburger Opernorchester. Dort schrieb er auch seine erste eigene Oper, die gleich ein großer Erfolg wurde. Er ging nach Italien, um die italienische Oper kennenzulernen, und dann nach London, wo er mit großem Erfolg 40 Opern komponierte. Aus einer dieser Opern stammt folgender Marsch.

Nach einem Bild von Hudson
gestochen von W. Bromley (1780)

Marsch der Perser

Georg Friedrich Händel 1685–1759
(aus der Oper „Floridante")
Satz: Xaver Poncette

Heute werden meistens Händels Kirchenwerke, wie zum Beispiel „Der Messias", aufgeführt. Aber auch seine Orchesterwerke, wie z.B. die „Wassermusik" und die „Feuerwerksmusik", sind sehr beliebt.

Die „Feuerwerksmusik" schrieb Händel für ein großes Feuerwerk, das in London am Ufer der Themse stattfand, um einen großen Friedensschluß zu feiern. Zu diesem Anlaß hatte der König sich nicht nur eine eigene Musik bestellt, sondern auch einen berühmten französischen Architekten engagiert, um ein großes hölzernes Gebäude zu errichten, von dem die aus Italien angereisten Spezialisten das Feuerwerk zünden sollten. Fast hätte dann das große Fest noch katastrophal geendet, denn einige Feuerwerkskörper setzten das Holzgebäude in Brand und viele Menschen flüchteten in Panik.

Händel führte seine Feuerwerksmusik an diesem Tag mit über 100 Bläsern auf. Später schrieb er dann die Fassung für Streicher und Bläser, die heute meistens gespielt wird und aus der das folgende Menuett stammt.

Königliches Feuerwerk 1749

Menuett aus der „Feuerwerksmusik"

Georg Friedrich Händel
Satz: Xaver Poncette

51

Der 2. Finger in C-Dur

82 a

Akzente mit Ab- und Aufstrich

In Vorbereitung auf die nächsten beiden Stücke spiele nun die Tonleiter mit kurzen Bogenstrichen und deutlichen Akzenten auf der ersten Note!

b

c

Tonleiter-Song

Kanon aus England

83

Wa - rum nur muß ich im - mer ü - ben die Ton - lei - ter, im - mer

Do, Re, Mi, Fa, Sol, Fa, Mi, Re,

Do, das nervt mich so, von Fa bis Do, ver - flix - tes „muß", das bringt Ver - druß!

Irische Jig

84

Die Jig ist ein alter englischer Volkstanz, den man heute noch in abgelegenen Gegenden Irlands antrifft. Die Jig wurde auch in die französische und deutsche Instrumentalmusik des Barock übernommen und heißt hier „Gigue".

Wenn du jemanden kennst, der Gitarre spielt, kann er dich mit den angegebenen Akkorden begleiten.
Vielleicht fällt dir auch eine eigene Begleitstimme für die Geige ein? Orientiere dich an den Buchstaben für die Gitarrenbegleitung.

Vorschlag für eine 2. Geigenstimme:

Als Komponist der 2. Stimme mußt du auch entscheiden, wie sie gespielt werden soll: *pizzicato* vielleicht, mit kurzen Strichen in der oberen Hälfte, mit Abstrichen am Frosch, oder vielleicht mit betonten ausgehaltenen No-

ten? Probiere die verschiedenen Möglichkeiten aus und schreibe deine Version in die Noten!
Auch das folgende Stück kommt aus Irland. Es ist ein altes Klagelied.

Londonderry Air

aus Irland
Satz: Mark Bruce

Wir wiederholen
den schwungvollen Aufstrich

Furiant – In der Küche zu singen

Melodie aus Böhmen

86

Spie - gel -ei, Ha-fer - brei, Toast Ha-wai, ko - chen heut Ka - si - mir und Kai

Erd - beer - eis, But - ter - reis, Kohl und Mais, kalt o - der - heiß.

Mar - me - la - de und Ap - fel - mus und Spa-ghet - ti im Ü - ber - fluß.

Al - ler - lei Lek - ke - rei, Schlek - ke-rei ko - chen die zwei.

Bedřich (Friedrich) Smetana, 1824–1884
(Zeichnung von Johann Lindner)

Der Furiant ist ein schneller, feuriger Volkstanz aus Böhmen. Typisch für ihn ist der „versteckte" Taktwechsel (2/4 und 3/4). Vielleicht begegnet dir diese Melodie einmal wieder: sie kommt in Friedrich Smetanas Oper „Die verkaufte Braut" vor.

Ouvertüre zur Oper „Die verkaufte Braut", 1866
(Smetanas Handschrift)

Menuett

Georg Philipp Telemann
1681–1767
Satz: Mark Bruce

87

Wir üben Pausen

Bona nox

Wolfgang Amadeus Mozart
1756–1791

88

Bo - na nox, bist a rech - ter Ochs; bo - na

not - te, lie - be Lot - te, bonne nuit. Pfui, pfui, good night, good

night, heut müaß ma no weit; gu-te Nacht gu-te Nacht, 's wird höchste Zeit, gu-te Nacht!

Schlaf fei g'sund und bleib recht ku - gel - rund!

Atte katte nuwa

Satz: Mark Bruce

89

At-te kat-te nu-wa, at-te kat-te nu-wa, e mi-sa de mi-sa

dul-la mi-sa de. He-xa kol-la mi-sa wo - - te,

he - xa kol-la mi-sa wo - te, at-te kat-te nu-wa,

at-te kat-te nu-wa, e mi-sa de mi-sa dul-la mi-sa de.

Ohren=vergnügendes und Gemüth=ergötzendes *

Tafel=CONFECT;

Bestehend

in 12. kurtzweiligen Sing=oder Tafel=Stucken
von 1. 2. oder 3. Stimmen/
mit einem CLAVIER, oder VIOLONCELLO
zu accompagniren,
Zur angenehmen Zeit=Vertreib
und
Aufmunterung melancholischen Humeurs
aufgetragen und vorgesetzt
Von einem Recht gut=meinenden Liebhaber.
Im Jahr,
VVo Man hIer fröLICh VnD LVstIg VVar.
CANTO I.

Zu finden bey Johann Jacob Lotter in Augspurg.

Das folgende Stück stammt aus dem „Augsburger Tafelkonfekt", einer Sammlung mit heiteren Musikstücken, die zur Unterhaltung während des Essens gedacht war. Zu dem Pausenstück gibt der Komponist folgende Spielanweisung: „In diesem Stück werden die Pausen das erste Mal mit Füßen getreten, das zweite Mal gepfiffen und das dritte Mal gelachet."

Pausenstück

Johann Valentin Rathgeber
1682–1750

90

Wir zählen Achtelnoten

Du weißt, daß am Anfang jedes Stückes die Taktart angegeben ist. Wenn du 4/4 oder C siehst, zählst du in jedem Takt vier Viertelnoten, wen du 6/8 siehst, zählst du sechs Achtelnoten und so weiter. Manchmal kann es aber auch sinnvoll sein, beim Zählen die Viertelnoten in Achtel zu unterteilen, besonders bei ruhigeren Stücken. Wir zählen dann: 1 und 2 und (3 und 4 und).

Sieh dir die beiden Andante von Haydn an! „Andante" heißt wörtlich „gehend" und ist eine Tempobezeichnung für ein ruhigeres Stück. Unsere beiden Andante werden in demselben Tempo gespielt, sind aber einmal im Vier-

viertel- und einmal im Zweivierteltakt notiert. Wenn wir in dem Zweivierteltakt „Achtel zählen", fällt es leichter, das Stück im langsamen Andante-Tempo zu spielen.

Das erste Andante ist der „St. Antonius-Choral" aus Haydns Divertimento Nr. 6, Johannes Brahms verwendete ihn als Thema für seine „Haydn-Variationen". Das zweite Andante stammt aus Haydns „Sinfonie mit dem Paukenschlag". Beide Stücke stammen aus berühmten Orchesterwerken; vielleicht kannst du sie dir einmal im Konzert oder auf einer Schallplatte anhören?

Andante

Joseph Haydn
1732–1809
Satz: Xaver Poncette

Andante

Joseph Haydn
aus der „Sinfonie mit dem Paukenschlag"
Satz: Xaver Poncette

ff = fortissimo = sehr laut

Haydn in London

Daß Joseph Haydn Hofkomponist beim Fürsten Esterhazy war, habe ich schon berichtet. Eines Tages bekam Haydn Besuch von Herrn Salomon aus London, der ihm eine Menge Geld versprach, wenn Haydn mit ihm nach London reisen und für Salomons Orchester Sinfonien schreiben würde. Damals gab es in London zwei Orchester, die öffentliche Konzerte gaben und um die Gunst des Publikums wetteiferten. Haydn bekam Urlaub von seinem Fürsten, und Salomon konnte ihn als den berühmten Wiener Komponisten in London vorstellen, wo er in den folgenden sechs Jahren mit seiner Musik riesigen Erfolg hatte. Haydn ließ sich aber auch immer neue Überraschungen einfallen, um das Londoner Publikum zu begeistern: so zum Beispiel die „Sinfonie mit dem Paukenschlag", die auf englisch Überraschungssinfonie („The Surprise") genannt wird.

Zu dieser Sinfonie erzählt man sich folgende Geschichte: In London ärgerte sich Haydn, daß viele vornehme Leute ins Konzert gingen, um ihre prächtigen Kleider zu zeigen, weniger um gute Musik zu hören. Er hatte sogar beobachtet, daß manche ein kleines Schläfchen hielten, besonders bei den langsamen Stücken. Die wollte er nun einmal richtig ärgern . . .

Piano beginnt das Andante der Paukenschlagsinfonie, friedlich und harmlos entwickelt es sich, so recht geeignet, dabei ein wenig zu schlummern. Da setzt mit einem Male das ganze Orchester mit einem kräftigen Fortissimo-Akkord ein, verstärkt durch einen lauten Paukenschlag. Entsetzt schrecken die Schläfer auf; mit dem ernstesten Gesicht dirigiert Haydn weiter, aber in seinen Augen sitzt der Schalk.

Wir komponieren

Das Thema aus Haydns „Andante" besteht aus einer Frage (Takt 1 und 2) und einer Antwort (Takt 3 und 4). Dieses Frage- und Antwortspiel kommt in der Musik oft vor. Denke nur an Lieder wie „Alle Vögel sind schon da" oder „Hänschen klein". Hier ist eine musikalische Frage für dich. Kannst du sie beantworten? Entsteht daraus ein kleines Musikstück?

Denke dir selber eine Frage und eine Antwort aus:

Auf den Erfinder des Metronoms

Kanon zu 4 Stimmen   Ludwig van Beethoven

1. + 3. Griffart

Das Metronom wurde von Beethovens Freund Johann Nepomuk Mälzel erfunden, der noch allerlei andere, heute vergessene „Musikmaschinen" konstruierte. Auf dem Metronom kannst du ein bestimmtes Tempo (z. B. Allegro) einstellen und hast dann eine Kontrolle, ob du dieses Tempo richtig einhälst. Bei M. M. = 60 (M. M. ist die Abkürzung für „Mälzels Metronom") tickt das Metronom genau 60mal in der Minute.

In seinem Kanon imitiert Beethoven das monotone Tikken des Metronoms, das einem manchmal wirklich ein bißchen auf die Nerven gehen kann... Auch im 2. Satz seiner 8. Sinfonie verwendet Beethoven diese Melodie. Spiele bitte den Kanon erst langsam und unterteile jedes Viertel in Achtelschläge.

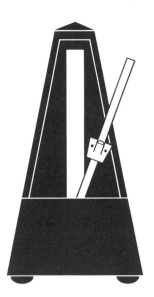

Triolen

Du weißt, daß die Viertelnote normalerweise in 2 Achtel eingeteilt wird. Wenn man sie in drei gleiche Teile aufteilt, erhält man eine Triole:

Triolenkanon

aus Frankreich

95

Bon - soir,   Bon - soir!   Ne- bel um-hül - let die Welt,

Nach - ti - gall sin - get ihr Lied.   Ne - bel um - hül - let die Welt,

Nach-ti - gall sin -get ihr Lied.   Bon - soir,   bon - soir!

Deutscher Text: Renate Bruce-Weber

Crescendo und decrescendo

Vorübung

Beginne im Piano mit wenig Bogen, nimm dann immer mehr, so daß der Ton zum Forte anschwillt, und werde mit immer kleineren Bogenstrichen wieder leiser! Spiele die Übung auf allen Saiten!

◁———▷	= crescendo (lauter werden)
▷———◁	= desrescendo (leiser werden)

96 *p* ———————————————————— *f* ———————————————————— *p*

Wie mußt du den Bogen bei dieser Übung einteilen?

f ———————————————————— *p* ———————————————————— *f*

Titelbild der Erstausgabe von Mozarts „Ein musikalischer Spaß" (1802)

Bei dem folgenden Spiegelkanon spielt der erste Geiger ganz normal von oben nach unten, während der zweite Geiger die Noten auf den Kopf stellt (wenn ihr das Heft flach zwischen euch hinlegt und gegenüber steht, könnt ihr beide aus denselben Noten spielen).

1. + 3. Griffart

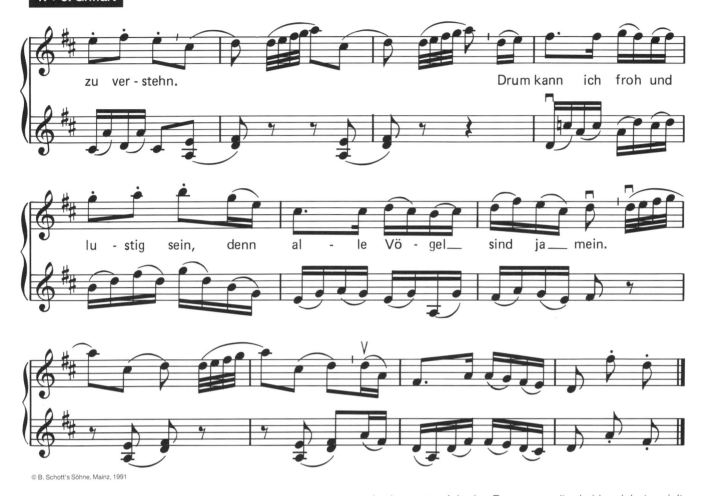

zu ver - stehn.　　Drum kann ich froh und

lu - stig sein, denn al - le Vö - gel__ sind ja__ mein.

♪ = Zweiunddreißigstelnote ♫♫ = ♪

𝄾 = Zweiunddreißigstelpause

In der ersten Arie des Papageno, die du hier siehst, spielt er kein Glockenspiel, sondern eine Panflöte. Viermal machst du auf deiner Geige diese Panflöte nach. Findest du die Stellen?

Noch einmal:
Doppelgriff-Training

Sextentonleiter

99

Kleine Doppelgriffetüde

100

Englischer Streitkanon

Henry Purcell
1659–1695

101

"He, ich bit - te dich, Freund-chen, strei-te nicht, sei schön fried-lich zu die - ser Stund'!"

"Schlin - gel, Schelm, Ha - lun - ke, du, jetzt hör mir, hör mir end - lich zu! Ich

ge - be mei-ne Mei-nung kund: Du bist zu rund!" "Ha, ha, ha, da lach ich nur, ver -

ach - te dich und blei -be stur, Spitz - bu - be, Gau-ner, bun-ter Hund, jetzt hal - te den Mund!"

Deutscher Text: Renate Bruce-Weber

Ein Kanon wie dieser wird auf englisch „Catch" genannt.
„Catch" heißt „fangen". Im Kanon müssen ja die nachfol-
genden Stimmen den Einsatz „fangen".
Zu Purcells Zeit gab es in England zahlreiche „Catch-
Clubs". Das waren Vereine, in denen vornehme Männer
sich trafen, um gesellige Abende mit Kanonsingen zu
verbringen.

Antonio Vivaldi

Antonio Vivaldi ist für uns Geiger ein wichtiger Name, denn er hat uns mehr als 200 (!) Violinkonzerte hinterlassen. Er lebte in Venedig und war Sohn eines Friseurs und Geigers. Diese Berufskombination war damals keineswegs unüblich, denn man pflegte in den Frisierstuben Musikinstrumente bereitzuhalten, mit denen sich die Kunden die Wartezeit vertreiben konnten.

Antonio Vivaldi selbst war zuerst Priester (wegen seiner roten Haare nannten ihn die Leute liebevoll „il prete rosso", d.h.: „der rote Priester"), wurde dann aber wegen einer Herzschwäche vom Lesen der Messe befreit und ging als Geigenlehrer an ein großes Mädchenwai-

senhaus. Diese Mädchen und jungen Damen bildeten ein Orchester, das unter Vivaldis Leitung bald sehr berühmt wurde und dessen Konzerte als Fremdenverkehrsattraktion galten. Für dieses Orchester schrieb Vivaldi seine „Concerti", nicht nur für Violine übrigens, sondern auch für Cello, Piccoloflöte, Trompete, Mandoline und Laute. Manche seiner Konzerte haben ein Motto, wie zum Beispiel die berühmten Violinkonzerte mit dem Titel „Die vier Jahreszeiten". Einen Auszug daraus, allerdings in etwas veränderter Form, haben wir hier abgedruckt. Es ist der Tanz der Bauern aus dem 3. Konzert „Der Herbst". Vivaldi schreibt dazu: „Der Bauer feiert mit Tänzen und Liedern das schöne Vergnügen der glücklichen Ernte."

Tanz der Bauern

Antonio Vivaldi
1678–1741
Bearbeitung: Xaver Poncette

Einführung in die 3. Lage

In dem Erster-Finger-Kletter-Walzer begegnet uns wieder einmal die Klettertonleiter. Der 1. Finger klettert hier nur bis zur 3. Lage, in der dann die anderen Finger die Melodie fortsetzen. In der 3. Lage mußt du die Töne mit einem anderen Finger greifen als in der 1. Lage. Deshalb stehen in diesem Stück Fingersätze über den Noten. Nach dem Walzer folgen viele Lieder und Stücke in der 3. Lage, zuerst ganz einfache, damit du dich langsam an die neue Lesart gewöhnen kannst. Alle Stücke verwenden die dritte Griffart – der 3. und 4. Finger liegen also nebeneinander.

Erster-Finger-Kletter-Walzer

Mark Bruce

3. Lage/2. Griffart

Die 3. Lage auf der D-Saite

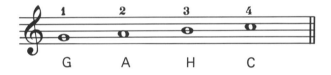

Suche dir, bevor du mit einem Lied oder Stück in der 3. Lage beginnst, über die Klettertonleiter den Anfangston:

Purzel rettet eine Maus (schon wieder!)

R. B-W.

104

Fing die Kat - ze ei - ne Maus, kam der Pur - zel grad nach Haus. Kläfft die

Kat - ze wü - tend an, daß die Maus ent - wi - schen kann.

Im Wiegeschritt

R. B-W.

105

Komm, wir tan - zen ei - nen Tanz im Wie - ge - schritt! Wer macht mit?

Die-ser Tanz im Wie - ge - schritt, der schun -kelt schön. Er wird ein Hit und hält fit.

Triumphmarsch

Renate Bruce-Weber
Satz: Mark Bruce

106

© B. Schott's Söhne, Mainz, 1991

Die 3. Lage auf der A-Saite

D   E   Fis   G

Vorübung

Lied von der alten Standuhr

R. B-W.

Wir ha - ben ei - ne al - te Uhr, die

tickt und tickt und tickt ganz stur, doch

vier - mal in der Stun - de, da setzt das Pen - del sich in — Gang und

horch: ein wun - der - schö - ner Klang er - freu - et uns - re — Run - de.

© B. Schott's Söhne, Mainz, 1991

Wir komponieren

Hier ist wieder ein Lied zum Vertonen. Bitte verwende die vorgegebenen Töne!

Glück! Glück! Glück! Glück! Heu - te hab' ich Glück!

Hab' den Schorn - stein - fe - ger auf dem Dach ge - se - hen.

Glück! Glück! Glück! Glück! Heu - te hab' ich Glück!

Text: Renate Bruce-Weber

2. (...) Habe einen Pfennig auf dem Hof gefunden.   *Erfinde weitere Strophen!*

Der „Canario" ist ein schneller Tanz im Dreiertakt und wurde im 17. Jahrhundert getanzt.

Canario

17. Jahrhundert
Satz: R. B-W.

Die 3. Lage auf der G-Saite

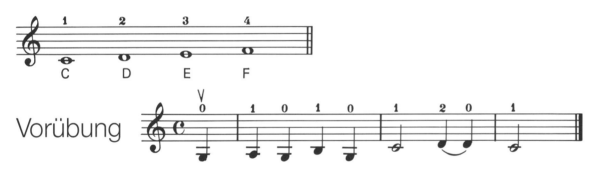

Vorübung

Der Bär und die Schnecke

R. B-W.

Langsam

110

Die-ser al-te Brum-mel-bär, der geht, der geht, der geht so schwer, die

Schneck', die ih-re Bah-nen zieht, ganz lang-sam nur sich fort-be-wegt. Der

dik-ke Bär, die klei-ne Schneck', in un-serm Lied da sind sie, sind sie, sind sie plötz-lich weg, weg, weg.

Bärentanz

R. B-W.

Der Baßgeiger dell'Occa
Zeichnung von E. T. A. Hoffmann

Lied des Baßgeigers

R. B-W.

Einiges zur Entwicklung der Geigensaiten

Die Geige hat vier Saiten. Das weiß jeder. Aber weißt du auch, aus was für Material deine Saiten hergestellt sind? Hast du auf deiner Geige Stahlsaiten (du erkennst sie an den Feinstimmern) oder Darmsaiten? Wir wollen uns hier etwas mit der Herstellung der hochwertigen Darmsaiten beschäftigen. Dies ist nämlich eine Kunst, und für die Geiger war es durchaus nicht immer selbstverständlich, daß sie gutklingende und verläßliche Saiten spielen konnten.

Saiten gibt es schon sehr, sehr lange in unserer Geschichte, denn für die uralten Saiteninstrumente, die in China oder im antiken Griechenland gespielt wurden, brauchte man ja auch schon Saiten. So gab es Saiten aus Seide, aus Hanf, sogar aus Roßhaar, aber auch schon aus Metall und aus Tierdärmen. Zur Entstehungszeit der Geige am Ende des 16. Jahrhunderts war die Saitenherstellung schon fortgeschritten, aber man experimentierte ständig weiter und entwickelte fortlaufend bessere.

Für die Herstellung von Darmsaiten verwendet man Därme von Schafen. Anfang des 18. Jahrhunderts brauchte man immerhin drei für eine E-Saite, sieben für eine G-Saite und 120 (!) für die dickste Saite des Kontrabasses. Heute schneidet man die Därme der Länge nach in Streifen und setzt die Saite aus vielen kleinen Teilen zusammen. Für die Herstellung der hochwertigen Saiten werden zunächst die Tiere sorgfältig ausgewählt: Man nimmt meist englische, möglichst magere Schafe, die im Alter von sechs bis acht Monaten geschlachtet werden. Dann beginnt der von Präzision bestimmte Herstellungsprozeß. Zuerst werden die Därme in einem chemischen Bad gereinigt, dann, wie erwähnt, in Streifen geschnitten. Diese werden gebleicht und zu einer Saite gedreht, die dann geschwefelt, getrocknet, poliert und rund gehobelt wird, bis sie gleichmäßig dick und glatt ist. Am Ende wird sie nochmals getrocknet.

Jetzt hast du dich vielleicht die ganze Zeit gewundert, daß die Darmsaiten, die wir heute verwenden, so gar nicht mehr nach Darm aussehen. Das kommt daher, daß man schon vor 200 Jahren, besonders um die Klangqualität der tiefen Saiten zu erhöhen, begonnen hat, die Saiten mit einem feinen Metalldraht zu umspinnen. Natürlich wird die Saite dadurch auch haltbarer. Lange Zeit hatten die Geiger besondere Probleme mit der E-Saite, weil die Darm-E-Saite sehr leicht riß. Daher mußten die Geiger die Violinkonzerte auch so üben, daß sie sie notfalls auch auf den unteren drei Saiten spielen konnten, um auf den Fall vorbereitet zu sein, daß im Konzert die E-Saite riß. Abhilfe brachte Anfang des 20. Jahrhunderts die Stahl-E-Saite, die zwar etwas schärfer klingt und etwas schwerer anspricht, aber sehr haltbar ist.

Nadine stimmt
ihre Geige schon allein.

3. Lage / 2. Griffart

Die 3. Lage auf der E-Saite

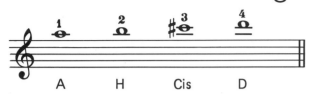

A H Cis D

Vorübung

Warten auf den Frühling

R. B-W.

Ju - belt, ju - belt all ihr Vö - ge - lein! Bald schon wird es wie - der

Früh - ling sein. Freut euch auf die er - sten war - men Son - nen-strah - len!

Seht, die Knos-pen sprie-ßen wie-der, hört die er-sten Früh-lings-lie - der! Ju - belt, ju - belt all!

Frühlingswalzer

Renate Bruce-Weber
Satz: Xaver Poncette

Marsch des Prinzen von Dänemark

Jeremiah Clarke
um 1673–1707
Satz: R. B-W.

115

Tonleiter-Scherz

Georg Philipp Telemann
1681–1767

116

Diese Fassung der G-Dur-Tonleiter stammt aus Telemanns Kantate „Der Schulmeister". Vielleicht wollte sich der Komponist hier ein wenig darüber lustig machen, daß alle Lehrer mit ihren Schülern immer und immer Tonleitern üben . . .

Das Echostück – in der 3. Lage

117

Sieh dir die ersten vier Takte von dem Echostück 2 an! Vergleiche sie mit den entsprechenden Takten aus dem Echostück 1! Erkennst du die Verwandtschaft?

Wir haben die Originaltakte an der mittleren Notenlinie „gespiegelt". Mit einem kleinen Handspiegel kannst du es leicht nachprüfen.

Magst du jetzt das Echostück 2 als Spiegelung zu Ende schreiben? Wie klingt es?

Echostück 2

Kanon

Adam Gumpelzhaimer
1559–1625

Englisches Abendlied

Satz: Xaver Poncette

120

Die C-Dur-Tonleiter in der 3. Lage

121

Spiele hierzu auch die Sechzehntel-Variante
(vergleiche S. 33).

Die kleine Eisenbahn – in der 3. Lage

122

accelerando

23 Die D-Dur-Tonleiter in der 3. Lage

Allegro

Renate Bruce-Weber
Satz: Xaver Poncette

24

© B. Schott's Söhne, Mainz, 1991

„Allegro" kommt, wie die meisten unserer musikalischen Fachbegriffe, aus dem Italienischen und bedeutet eigentlich soviel wie „fröhlich" oder „heiter". Es hat aber als Tempobezeichnung die Bedeutung „schnell" erhalten.

3. Lage / 2. Griffart

Aus der „Bauern-Kantate" – in der 3. Lage

Johann Sebastian Bach
1685–1750
Bearbeitung: Mark Bruce

125

Wir improvisieren

Hast du einen Freund oder eine Freundin, die auch Geige spielen? Oder habt ihr vielleicht sogar manchmal zusammen Unterricht? Dann freut ihr euch sicherlich, daß ihr so viele schöne Duette in diesem Kapitel zweistimmig musizieren könnt.

Habt ihr auch schon einmal probiert, eure eigene Musik zu spielen? So ganz ohne Noten? Ihr könnt allerlei Spiele erfinden. Hier sind einige Vorschläge:

1. Stellt euch Rücken an Rücken. Einer denkt sich eine kurze Melodie aus und der andere spielt sie nach.

2. Nehmt ein bekanntes Kinderlied und spielt es abwechselnd Zeile für Zeile, z. B. „Kommt ein Vogel geflogen".:

> Kommt ein Vogel geflogen,
> setzt sich nieder auf mein Fuß,
> hat ein Zettel im Schnabel,
> von der Mutter einen Gruß.

Dann denkt euch zu dem Text eure eigene Melodie aus! Wenn ihr euch wieder zeilenweise abwechselt, hört gut zu, was der andere gespielt hat, und versucht, musikalisch darauf zu antworten.

3. Oder ihr „unterhaltet" euch auf euren Geigen mit frei erfundenen „Fragen und Antworten" (siehe Nr. 93).

Wenn man ohne Noten nach der eigenen Eingebung musiziert, nennt man das „Improvisieren".

Alte Tanzweise

17. Jahrhundert
Satz: Xaver Poncette

Volkstanz aus Holland

Satz: Xaver Poncette

Ein Virtuosenstück – leicht gemacht

Niccolo Paganini, den großen Violinvirtuosen, kennst du schon. Er ist berühmt dafür, daß seine Stücke im Schwierigkeitsgrad an die Grenzen der Geigentechnik reichen. Sein „Allegretto" haben wir etwas verändert, damit du es spielen kannst. In Paganinis Original werden die erste und zweite Stimme von *einem* Geiger in Doppelgriffen gespielt, allerdings ohne die leere D-Saite und in einer anderen Tonart (siehe S. 110).

Niccolo Paganini
Holzschnitt v. Albert Edouard

Allegretto

Niccolo Paganini
1782–1840
Satz: R. B.-W.

Dreiklänge in der 3. Lage

129

Weißt du, wie diese Dreiklänge heißen?

Menuett

Johann Philipp Kirnberger
1721–1783
Satz: Xaver Poncette

130

J. Ph. Kirnberger war Schüler von Johann Sebastian Bach.

Scherzando

Daniel Gottlob Türk
1750–1813
Satz: R. B-W.

31

Schützenmarsch

132

Englischer Volkstanz

Satz: Xaver Poncette

133

Wir verbinden
die ersten drei Griffarten

Mit den Tönen der ersten drei Griffarten kannst du nun auch Molltonleitern spielen.

Anders als bei der Durtonleiter gibt es bei der Molltonlei-ter drei verschiedene Formen. Schau dir bitte die erste, die „reine" oder „natürliche" Molltonleiter an und markiere die Halbtonschritte mit diesem Zeichen: ⌒

Die reine Molltonleiter

34

Die harmonische Molltonleiter

35

Der reinen Molltonleiter fehlt der Leitton. Um wieder ein starkes Grundtongefühl herzustellen, hat man bei der harmonischen Molltonleiter den 7. Ton als „Leitton" er-höht. Welches Intervall entsteht dadurch zwischen dem 6. und 7. Ton der Tonleiter?

Es ist die „übermäßige" Sekunde.

Die melodische Molltonleiter

36

Da der Schritt vom f zum gis schwer zu singen (und zu spielen) ist, hat man noch eine „melodischere" Fassung der Molltonleiter erfunden. Hier ist auch der 6. Ton er-höht, allerdings nur in der Aufwärtsbewegung. Abwärts geht die melodische Molltonleiter wie die reine Molltonlei-ter (man könnte sie sonst leicht mit Dur verwechseln).

In welcher Tonart steht dieses Lied?

Hinunter ist der Sonnenschein

Melodie: Melchior Vulpius, 1609

137

Kannst Du dieses Stück auch in Dur spielen? Welcher Ton ändert sich in der Melodie?

Französischer Kontratanz

17. Jahrhundert
Satz: Xaver Poncette

138

1., 2. + 3. Griffart

Der hat vergeben

Johann Valentin Rathgeber
1682–1750
aus: „Augsburger Tafelkonfekt"
Satz: Mark Bruce

39

Der hat ver - ge - ben das e - wig Le - ben, der nicht die Mu - sik liebt
Wer hier auf Er - den will se - lig wer - den, der kann er - rei - chen hie

und sich be - stän - dig übt in __ die - sem __ Spiel. Es gibt der
durch Mu - sik __ oh - ne Müh sein __ letz - tes __ Ziel.

Fine

höch - ste Gott den Eng - lein dies Ge - bot: Es sin - ge Che - ru - bim,

es sin - ge Se - ra - phim der __ Eng - lein __ viel.

D. C. al Fine

Noch einmal:
Crescendo und decrescendo

Hat dir das Crescendo Spaß gemacht? Wir wollen es noch einmal probieren und wiederholen zunächst Übung 96.

Haydn und Mozart beim Musizieren (Glasmalerei)

Das folgende Lied von J. Haydn wurde so für zwei Geigen eingerichtet, daß die 1. Geige teilweise die Haupt- und teilweise die Begleitstimme spielt.
Spiele an den Begleitstellen leise und höre der Melodiestimme zu!

Der wahrlich schlaue Hund

Joseph Haydn
Satz: Mark Bruce

Zwei Freun - de, Se - bald und Pe - trill, von ei - nem gu - ten Stan - de, die

zo - gen, wie man mel - den will, ver - gnüg - lich durch die Lan - de.

Pe -

140

1., 2. + 3. Griffart

Textnachdichtung: Renate Bruce-Weber

Dieses Lied von Joseph Haydn hat viele Strophen und erzählt eine lustige Geschichte:

2. So groß sei sein Verstande gar
daß er ohn Müh könnt finden
dieses silbern Geldstück hier fürwahr,
versteckt man's bei der Linden.
Die Wette galt; gesagt, getan.
Der Weg ward fortgesetzt sodann.

3. Indessen zu der Linden kam ein
junges Handwerksbürschchen,
war froh und ohne Sorg und Gram,
dacht still nur an sein Liebchen.
Da fühlt er zwischen Gras und Moos:
„Was ist das für ein Geldstück bloß?"

4. Er lobt das Glück und den Verstand
und läßt das Silber blinken.
„Das hat Fortuna mir gesandt" –
läßt's in sein Säcklein sinken.
Nach Stunden Weile kam der Hund
und suchte nach: weg war der Fund.

5. Was tat der Hund? Er kam und sah
doch nicht mehr als ein Blinder;
ein Mensch stünd ohne Rat nun da,
der Hund verfolgt den Finder.
Er war so schlau, so ungestüm,
gesellt ganz freundlich sich zu ihm.

6. „Geld und auch einen schönen Hund?
Das Glück muß für mich wachen."
So sprach und fing aus Herzensgrund
der Jüngling an zu lachen.
„Du Pudel bist zwar nicht für mich,
allein verkaufen kann ich dich.

7. Bis in die Herberg war's nicht weit,
der Bursch und Pudel bleiben
dort eine ganze Nacht zu zweit.
Was mag der Pudel treiben?
Indes das Geldstück lag bedeckt
von unsres Burschen Hos versteckt.

8. Kaum geht zum Wecken dann die Tür,
sieht man den Pudel eilen,
nimmts Säckel, Geld und Hos sogar
und läuft schnell zu den Seinen. –
Dies Lied ist da, euch zu erbaun
und lehrt, dem Glücke nicht zu traun!

95

Gullivers Reise zu den Liliputanern

Telemann war ein humorvoller Mensch. So komponierte
er Gullivers Reise zu den Zwergen, den „Liliputanern", im
3/32-Takt. Nun erschrick nicht: Es ist ein eher langsames
Stück, eine Chaconne.
Damit du es besser lesen kannst, haben wir es zusätzlich
in einen 3/4-Takt übertragen. Das Stück sieht dann viel
leichter aus (vgl. S. 97).

Georg Philipp Telemann

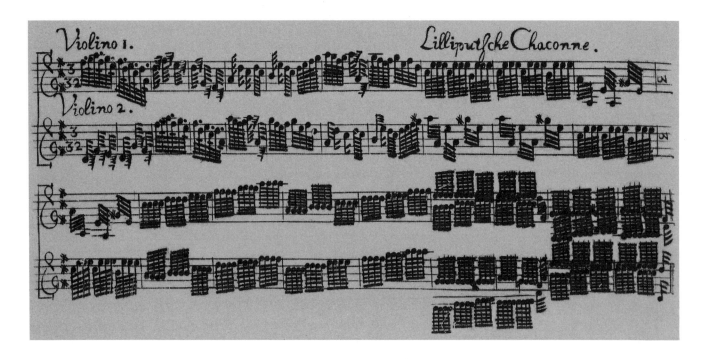

Liliput-Chaconne. Aus Telemanns Sammlung „Der getreue Musicmeister" (1728)

1., 2. + 3. Griffart

Gullivers Reise zu den Liliputanern – im ¾-Takt

Georg Philipp Telemann

Menuett

Georg Philipp Telemann
1681–1767
Satz: Mark Bruce

142

Wir verbinden die 1. und 3. Lage

In den folgenden Liedern und Stücken kommen die 1. und die 3. Lage vor. Mit dem Lied „Wir sind die Musikanten" geht's ganz leicht los: Durch die Pausen hast du viel Zeit, die Lage zu wechseln. Achte von nun an ganz besonders auf die angegebenen Fingersätze, damit du weißt, was in der 1. und was in der 3. Lage gespielt werden soll.

Wir sind die Musikanten

Volkslied
Satz: Mark Bruce

Wir sind die Mu-si-kan-ten und komm'n aus Schwa-ben-land. Wir sind die Mu-si-kan-ten und

komm'n aus Schwa-ben-land. Wir kön-nen spie-len Vi-o, Vi-o, Vi-o-lin.

Wir kön-nen spie-len Baß, Vi-ol und Flöt. Und wir könn'n tan-zen hop-sas-sa,

hop-sas-sa, hop-sas-sa, und wir könn'n tan-zen hop-sas-sa, hop-sas-sas-sa!

Der Lagenwechsel über die leere Saite

Damit du nun auch ohne Pausen schnell und mühelos zwischen der 1. und 3. Lage wechseln kannst, wollen wir uns im Folgenden etwas intensiver mit dem Lagenwechsel befassen. Der „Lagenwechsel" ist dir ja nicht neu. Du bist schon öfter in die Lagen „geklettert" und auch schon „gerutscht". Weißt du noch, was der Unterschied ist? „Klettern", also den Finger hochnehmen und in der neuen Lage aufsetzen, kannst du nur, wenn eine leere

Saite zwischen dem Lagenwechsel steht. Ansonsten mußt du **immer** „rutschen", das heißt den Finger auf der Saite liegenlassen.
Beginnen wir mit dem Lagenwechsel über die leere Saite. Den „Ausflug" und den „Schwungtanz" kennst du schon aus dem ersten Band der „Fröhlichen Violine" Achte jetzt jedoch auf den angegebenen Fingersatz in der 1. und 3. Lage!

Übung

144

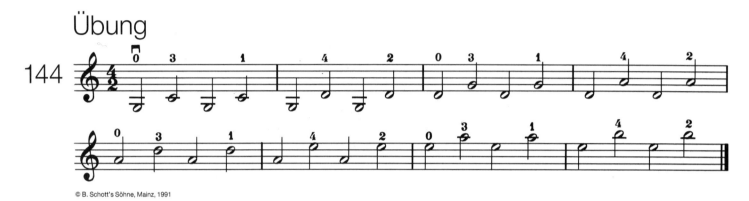

Der Ausflug

R. B-W.

145

Komm! wir ma-chen ei-nen Aus-flug nach Ti - ra - ti - rusch-ka - ka mit dem Va-ter und der Mut-ter und der al-ten Ba-busch-ka. Nach Ti - rusch-ka - ka mit der Ba - busch-ka.

Fällt dir zu diesem Lied eine Begleitstimme ein?

Schwungtanz

R. B-W.

146

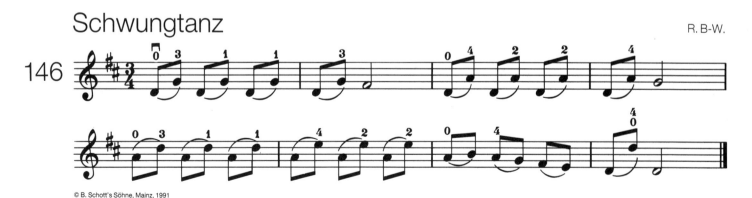

Titelbild von Leopold Mozarts Violinschule (1756)

Wolfgang Amadeus Mozart
aus dem
„Londoner Skizzenbuch" (1764)
Bearbeitung: R.B-W.

Allegretto

Wettlauf zur Hochzeit

Jig aus Irland

148

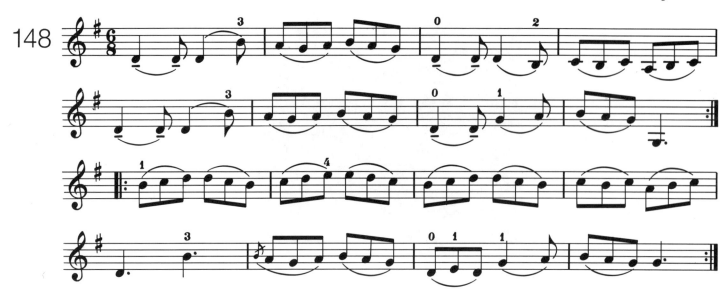

— Der Lagenwechsel mit demselben Finger —

Da die meisten Stücke keine leere Saite zwischen dem Lagenwechsel haben, folgen nun Übungen zum Rutschen. Bitte rutsche immer zuerst langsam! Den Lagenwechsel darf man ruhig hören.

Rutschbahn 1

149

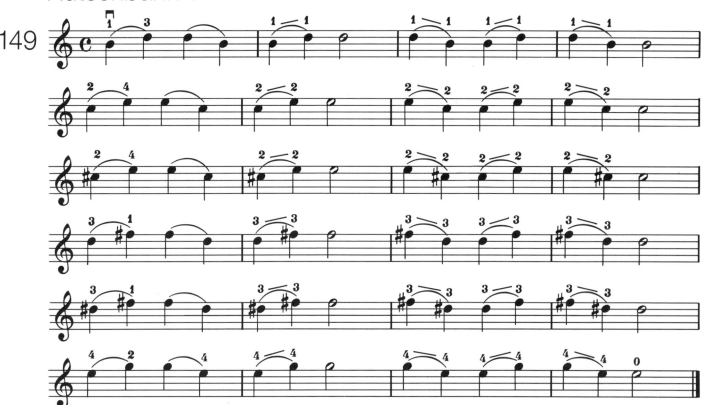

Der Rutscher
(Pfälzischer Paartanz)

Satz: Xaver Poncette

The last Jig
Zeichnung von Thomas Rowlandson, 1818

103

Träumerei

R. B-W.

151

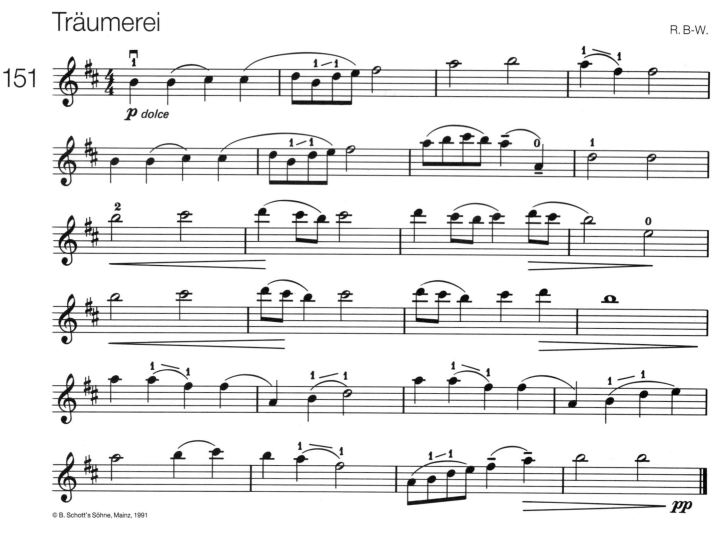

Die Ausdrucksbezeichnung „dolce" bedeutet: weich, zart oder süß.

pp = pianissimo = sehr leise

Schlittschuhwalzer

R. B-W.
Satz: Mark Bruce

152

1. + 3. Lage

Notensinfonie
Zeichnung von Moritz v. Schwind
(1804–1871)

Der Schrägstrich beim Fingersatz, zum Beispiel ⸝³ bedeutet, daß der Rutscher hörbar sein soll. Setze deshalb den Finger schon in der 1. Lage auf und spiele, als wenn ein kurzer Vorschlag notiert wäre:

Katzenkanon

aus Frankreich

153

Mi - au, mi - au! Hörst du mich schrei-en, mi - au, mi - au, ich will dich frei - en!

Folgst du mir aus dei - nen Ge-mä-chern, sin - gen wir___ hoch auf den Dä - chern

Mi - au, komm, ge-lieb-te Kat - ze, mi - au, reich mir dei-ne Tat - ze!

Deutscher Text: Liselotte Holzmeister
aus: „Der Zündschlüssel", Fidula-Verlag, Boppard/Rhein

Samba

1. + 3. Lage

aus Mexico
Satz: Xaver Poncette

54

Holt eu-re In-stru-men - te! Wir fah-ren zu dem Pan - cho. Der

hat ein' gro-ßen Ran - cho. Da fei-ern wir ein Fest.___ Wir es-sen En-cha-

la - da und tan-zen ei - nen Sam - ba. Weit tönt es durch die

Pam - pa: Will - komm' in Me-xi - ko!___ Me - xi - ko!___

Deutscher Text: Renate Bruce-Weber

Der Lagenwechsel
zwischen dem 1. und 2. Finger

Oft kommt der Lagenwechsel innerhalb einer Tonleiter-folge vor. Auch hier muß der Finger rutschen.
Spiele zum Üben zuerst den Rutscher mit (wie notiert).

Später soll in Aufwärtsrichtung der 1. den 2. Finger und in Abwärtsrichtung der 2. den 1. Finger so schnell weg-schieben, daß man den Lagenwechsel nicht mehr hört.

Vorübung

155

Ist ein Mann in' Brunn' gefallen

156

Ist ein Mann in' Brunn' ge - fal - len, hab' ihn hö - ren plump - sen,

wär' ich nicht hin - zu - ge - kom - men, wär' der Mann er - trun - ken.

Ferienlied – in der 1. und 3. Lage

Spiele auch das „Ferienlied" zuerst langsam und mit einem deutlichen Rutscher!

R. B-W.

157

Fe - rien! Fe - rien! Wir woll'n ei - ne Rei - se ma - chen, Va - ter holt den

Wa - gen. Packt schnell eu - re Sie - ben - sa - chen! Ich kann nicht mehr war - ten.

Nicht ver - ges - sen: Tau - cher - bril - le, Ba - de - ho - se, An - gel - ha - ken; Gei - ge, No - ten,

Zahn - putz - zeug, den Haus - hund und ein Ba - de - la - ken. Fe - rien! Fe - rien!

Rutschbahn 2

58

Rutschbahn 3

59

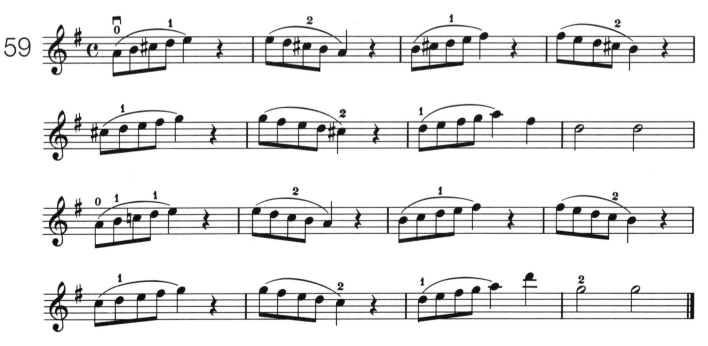

Banditenlied

Renate Bruce-Weber
Satz: Xaver Poncette

161 Allegretto von Paganini

Spiele jetzt bei diesem Stück (Nr. 128)
die zweite Stimme.

College Hornpipe

England, um 1850
Satz: Mark Bruce

Der Lagenwechsel
auf der gleichen Note

Charaktervariationen

Thema (Tempo di Minuetto)

Mark Bruce

163

Var. 1 (Allegro)

pizz.

pizz.

arco

pizz.

arco

© B. Schott's Söhne, Mainz, 1991

Var. 2 (Trauermarsch) Langsam und feierlich

Finale (Walzer)

Behalte beim Pizzicato in Variation 1 den Bogen in der Hand!

Lagenwechsel bunt gemischt

Viel Spaß mit den nächsten drei Liedern, deren „Lagenwechselspielchen" sich aus dem Text ergeben! In diesem Lied wird das Wort „Maus" beziehungsweise „Mausemaus" immer mit dem 1. Finger gespielt.

Erster-Finger-Mausesong

Volkslied
Satz: Xaver Poncette

Der Kuckuck – in der 3. Lage

Text: Friedrich Rückert
Melodie: Ernst Schmid
Satz: Xaver Poncette

Hier erklingt der Kuckucksruf immer in der 3. Lage.

Aus: Musik und Tanz für Kinder, Die Tripptrappmaus, ED 7236
© B. Schott's Söhne, Mainz, 1984

Im nächsten Lied gibt es viele Texteinschübe. Durch den Wechsel zwischen der 1. und 3. Lage und dem damit verbundenen Klangfarbenunterschied kommen sie auch auf der Geige deutlich heraus. Du darfst sogar die Kommas mitspielen und die kleine Kommapause für den Lagenwechsel benutzen.

Hätt ich nur recht viel Geld

Böhmisches Volkslied
Satz: Xaver Poncette

Hätt' ich nur, ihr lie - ben Mäd-chen, recht viel, *lie - be Mäd-chen,* recht viel, *lie - be Mäd-chen,*

recht viel Geld, hätt ich ei - ne schö-ne Mu-sik bald be -, *schö-ne Mu-sik,* bald be -,

schö - ne Mu-sik, bald be - stellt! Will die Mu - sik spie-len las - sen wie mein Lieb mich

hat ver - las - sen und ich, *ja, mein Mäd-chen,* und ich, *ja, mein Mäd-chen,* und ich dich.

Moderato

Josef Bodin de Boismortier
1691–1755

167

Fine

D.C. al Fine

Allemanda

Felice de Giardini
1716–1796

La Rejouissance

Georg Friedrich Händel
aus der „Feuerwerksmusik"
Bearbeitung: Xaver Poncette

Flötenkonzert am Hofe Friedrichs des Großen
Federzeichnung v. Adolph von Menzel

Ein König der komponiert? Ja, das gibt es: Friedrich II. (der Große), König von Preußen (1712–1786). Sein Lehrer war der bekannte Flötist Johann Joachim Quantz (1697–1733).

Aus den Flötenübungen Friedrichs des Großen

Lieder
für besondere Anlässe

Happy Birthday to You

171

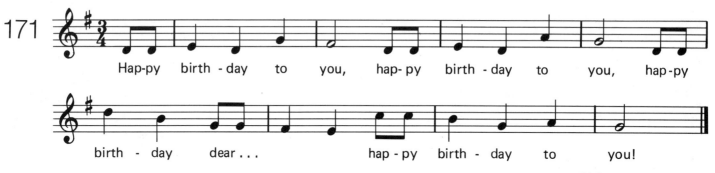

Hap-py birth-day to you, hap-py birth-day to you, hap-py

birth-day dear... hap-py birth-day to you!

Geburtstagsmarsch

Renate Bruce-Weber
Satz: Mark Bruce

172

Kom-met all und laßt uns brin-gen un-ser

Ständ-chen, spie-len, sin-gen, gra-tu-lie-ren mit Mu-

sik, wün-schen Se-gen, Freud und Glück.

2. Stimmet eure Instrumente,
spielet fein und „dolcemente",
daß dies schöne Lied gelingt,
kräftig und von Herzen klingt.

Hochzeitsmarsch

Felix Mendelssohn-Bartholdy
1809–1847
aus: Ein Sommernachtstraum
Bearbeitung: Mark Bruce

Sankt Martin

aus dem Rheinland
Satz: Mark Bruce

174

Sankt Mar - tin, Sankt Mar - tin, Sankt Mar - tin ritt durch Schnee und _ Wind, sein Roß, das trug ihn fort ge - schwind. Sankt Mar - tin ritt mit leich - tem Mut, sein Man - tel deckt ihn warm und gut.

2. | : Im Schnee saß, : | im Schnee da saß ein armer Mann,
hatt Kleider nicht, hatt Lumpen an.
„Oh helft mir doch in meiner Not,
sonst ist der bittre Frost mein Tod!"

3. | : Sankt Martin, : | Sankt Martin zieht die Zügel an,
das Roß steht still beim armen Mann.
Sankt Martin mit dem Schwerte teilt
den warmen Mantel unverweilt.

4. | : Sankt Martin, : | Sankt Martin gibt den halben still,
der Bettler rasch ihm danken will.
Sankt Martin aber ritt in Eil
hinweg mit seinem Mantelteil.

Neujahrswunsch

Johann Valentin Rathgeber
aus dem „Augsburger Tafelkonfekt"
Satz: Mark Bruce

75

Ein glück-se-ligs Jahr! Dies wol-len wir wün-schen den Klei-nen und

Gro-ßen. Es ist ja vom Glück-wunsch kein Mensch aus-ge - schlos-sen. Wir

wün - schen's ei - nem je - den,__ wer's im - mer__ sein__

soll, habn's al - le__ ver - die - net, ihr__ wis - set's ja__

wohl. Ja gelt, das ist wahr? Ein glück - se - ligs Jahr!

— Übersicht der Stricharten —

Die Ziffern beziehen sich auf die Nummern der Stücke.

Lieder und Spielstücke

WHAT'S AT ISSUE?

RICH OR POOR

Jeremy Wallis

www.heinemann.co.uk/library
Visit our website to find out more information about **Heinemann Library** books.

To order:
 Phone 44 (0) 1865 888066
 Send a fax to 44 (0) 1865 314091
💻 Visit the Heinemann Bookshop at www.heinemann.co.uk/library to browse our catalogue and order online.

First published in Great Britain by Heinemann Library, Halley Court, Jordan Hill, Oxford OX2 8EJ, a division of Reed Educational and Professional Publishing Ltd. Heinemann is a registered trademark of Reed Educational & Professional Publishing Limited.

OXFORD MELBOURNE AUCKLAND JOHANNESBURG BLANTYRE
GABORONE IBADAN PORTSMOUTH NH (USA) CHICAGO

Designed by Tinstar Design (www.tinstar.co.uk)
Illustrations by Nicholas Beresford-Davies
Originated by Ambassador Litho Ltd
Printed in Hong Kong/China

ISBN 0 431 03556 3   (hardback)   ISBN 0 431 03564 4   (paperback)
06 05 04 03 02   06 05 04 03 02
10 9 8 7 6 5 4 3 2   10 9 8 7 6 5 4 3 2 1

British Library Cataloguing in Publication Data
Wallis, Jeremy
    Rich or poor. – (What's at issue?)
    1. Wealth – Juvenile literature 2. Poverty – Juvenile literature
    3. Wealth – Regional disparities – Juvenile literature
    I. Title
    306.3

Acknowledgements
The Publishers would like to thank the following for permission to reproduce photographs:
AKG: p6; Corbis: p28, Hulton-Deutsch p4, Bettmann pp7, 39, 40, Howard Davies p11, Jennie Woodcock p14, Jon Spaull p15, Penny Tweedie p16, Kevin Fleming pp18, 27, Dave G Houser p24, Daniel Laine p25, Brian Harding p32, Jonathan Blair p34, Dean Conger p41, AFP p42; Cumulus: Steve Benbow: p30, Library of Congress p36, pp37, 38; John Birdsall: pp12, 26; Rex Features: p31, Sipa Press p8, 21, David Browne p10; Stone:John Millar: p22.

Cover photograph: Report Digital.

Our thanks to Julie Turner (Head of Student Services and SENCO, Banbury School, Oxfordshire) for her comments in the preparation of this book.

Every effort has been made to contact copyright holders of any material reproduced in this book. Any omissions will be rectified in subsequent printings if notice is given to the Publisher.

Any words appearing in the text in bold, **like this**, are explained in the Glossary.

Contents

Introduction

'One for you, one for me...'

As children, we are encouraged to share and share alike, something we learn with brothers, sisters, or our friends in the playground. But in the modern world wealth, possessions and **resources** are not shared equally. Many things – access to education, career opportunities, health care – are dependent on wealth.

How have extremes of wealth and poverty developed? Why is it that, as nations have grown richer, the way money is shared within them actually becomes more unequal? Why have some nations got poorer, and others richer? Are we as individuals at fault for our own circumstances or are they caused by factors beyond our control? This book examines some of the arguments and facts to help you make up your own mind.

Rich or poor – a modern argument?

There are many questions about how wealth is divided, and many complicated arguments surround the issue. Some have been going on for thousands of years! In Ancient Greece, an Athenian ruler called Solon introduced a **democratic** system to balance the rich and the poor. Years later, the philosopher Plato said this was still the main cause of conflict in Athens.

'Democracy,' argued one Greek aristocrat, 'is a device for exploiting the rich and putting money into the pockets of the poor.' Inequality was a theme often used by the Greek dramatists.

A divided history: schoolboys outside gates of Lord's cricket ground during the Eton v Harrow match, 1937.

Two arguments

By the end of the 5th century BC, political thought had taken two main directions. One saw both nature and human beings as social and cooperative. The second said people were instinctively selfish and only interested in themselves.

The debate about how **resources** should be divided has been going on ever since. At its root is an argument about who we are as social beings and how we behave towards others. Today, some people argue for a more equal distribution of wealth because they believe it is morally wrong to allow a few to control too much wealth. They also argue that it is in everyone's interest to share the world's resources more equally.

Opponents of this argument claim the accumulation of wealth is natural and desirable. They say those with **innate** abilities – for business, sport, or singing, who are more beautiful or have more interesting things to say – should benefit from them. Some also claim the poor will always be poor, because poverty is built into people's behaviour, culture and character, that it is culturally or genetically predetermined. They think we should do nothing to interfere with the way wealth is shared out.

But others ask that if poverty is culturally or genetically predetermined, why do the numbers affected by poverty change so much over short periods of time? They argue that it is changing circumstances that cause poverty, and we must consider the welfare of all and find ways to reduce the bad effects of change.

Winners and losers

Those who believe in inequality say we have no duty to anyone but our families and ourselves, even claiming there is no such thing as 'society'. People are naturally competitive, they argue. Competition frees the most creative and intelligent aspects of our personalities. To have winners there must be losers and no one should be held back.

In the 2500 years since the time of the Ancient Greeks, wealth, poverty and inequality has provoked furious, sometimes violent, argument. The way riches have been distributed has stimulated the spread of religions such as Christianity; provoked revolutions like those in France, Russia, Mexico, Germany, Cuba, China; civil wars in England, Spain, the United States; independence struggles in Latin America, Ireland, Italy, throughout Africa and Asia; strikes and undemocratic movements around the world. Watching TV, it becomes obvious how many newsworthy events – elections, riots, wars, revolutions, civil wars, and military takeovers – are linked to the distribution of wealth. Why do you think these debates about 'who gets what' become so fierce? What do you think might happen if inequality gets worse? When resources become scarce or more expensive, will they become another source of conflict? Is extreme inequality an issue we should tackle now to stop more terrible conflicts in the future and protect the welfare of future generations? What efforts have people made to reduce inequality? Or is inequality something beyond our control – like the work of a giant, invisible hand – that we cannot, in the long term, do anything about?

Wealth and social class

Grouping people by social rank, or class, is as old as society itself. Sometimes it is by religion or race – an example is the caste system in India. Social differences are shown by the caste each Indian is born into. The Brahmin or priest caste is at the top while the so-called 'untouchables' are at the bottom. Based on the idea of reincarnation (rebirth), caste membership is seen as a consequence of conduct in the previous life.

Workers and aristocracy

Grouping people according to where they fit in society has often been done according to wealth. The independent cities of Ancient Greece were divided into distinct social classes. The majority were tradesmen and artisans (skilled workers) whose lives could be very insecure. There was a small, wealthy **aristocracy**. Extremes of wealth and poverty ensured that **democratic** life in the city was fiery and sometimes violent.

Patricians and plebs

In Ancient Rome, politics was also about rich and poor – between the aristocracy (patricians) and the common people (plebeians). Many famous Roman rulers kept the favour of the people by providing 'bread and games'. Christianity found its first believers among the very poorest subjects of the Roman **Empire**.

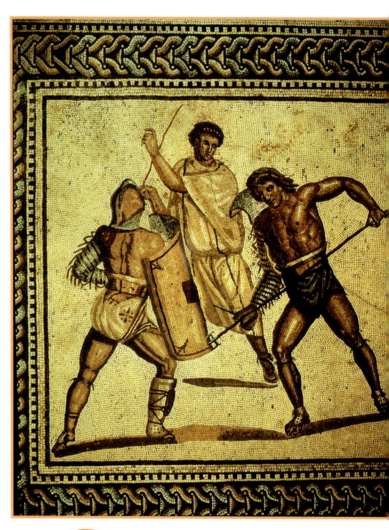

The Roman Games were used to keep the poor majority of Roman citizens happy.

Peasants and nobles

In Medieval Europe, wealth was based on land. The feudal system meant that everyone from peasant to noble to monarch owed their living to the person above and had a debt of service to them. (The monarch, it was believed, owed his power to God.) Violent upheavals often threatened the feudal system, for instance, the Peasants' Revolt in England.

George Orwell, author of *1984* and *Animal Farm*, called England 'the most class-ridden country in the world'.

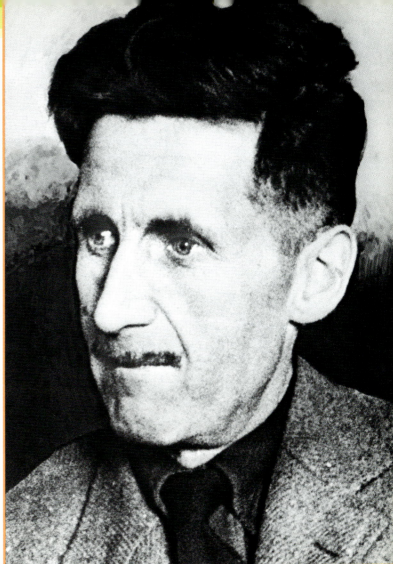

These **uprisings** were often religious, predicting a 'Heaven on Earth' where wealth was abolished and land held equally by all. They usually occurred during times of natural calamity such as the Black Death (a plague that swept through Europe and Asia in the 14th century) or periods of high unemployment, when people's fears were strongest.

Many people have tried to define what puts a person in a particular 'class'. Is it just wealth? Or a combination of things – accent, where a person lives, income, occupation? Some people think it is the difference between those who eat 'dinner and tea' and those who eat 'lunch and dinner'! While there is no generally agreed definition of social class, and some politicians argue there is 'no such thing as class' or that we are 'classless', everyone agrees that social division exists.

SOCIAL MOBILITY

In modern industrial societies, class division is less rigid. People have 'social mobility', which means they can, over generations or even their own lifetime, move up the social scale. Ask your parents or grandparents what *their* grandparents did and where they came from. It is an interesting way of charting social mobility from a personal point of view.

FACT

Every ten years the British Government carries out a census or count of the population. It classes people according to how they fit one of seven occupational groups:

I   Professional occupations
II Managerial and technical occupations
III N Skilled non-manual occupations
III M Skilled manual occupations
IV Partly-skilled occupations
V   Unskilled occupations
VI Armed forces

Because of changes in the way people work and in society, this system is being reviewed.

A world of rich and poor

To many people growing up in a **developed country**, the world is alive with possibilities. It is easy to be swept up in the excitement of new technology, the Internet and **e-commerce**. But don't forget – the world is harshly divided. Even in Britain there is a gulf between wealth and need. Only in New Zealand have income inequalities widened more than in Britain since 1980.

There are millions throughout the world for whom life is a struggle; where family and social relationships are shaped by poverty; where extremes of wealth and hardship create crime, illness and war; where life, as the English philosopher Thomas Hobbes said, is 'nasty, brutish and short'.

RICH FACTS

There are individuals so rich they can change the economic balance of nations. They can control media and governments, buy entire football teams or control sporting competitions. There are sports personalities and pop-stars better known for their wealth and lavish lifestyles than for their prowess on pitch or stage.

- According to War on Want, the richest 20 per cent of the world's people now receive over 150 times more income than the poorest 20 per cent.

- There are 358 dollar-billionaires in the world.

- The world's three richest billionaires have **assets** greater than the total economic output of the least developed countries and their 600 million people.

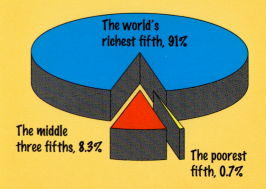

The world's richest fifth, 91%

The middle three fifths, 8.3%

The poorest fifth, 0.7%

The real distribution of wealth amongst all people. Chart from War on Want.

Conflict and poverty go hand in hand: years of war have ruined the lives of many people in South East Asia. This child soldier is a member of the rebel army of the Kampuchean Khmer Rouge.

What is poverty?

The **World Bank** defines poverty as lacking the money needed to obtain minimum levels of food, clothing and shelter. Anyone earning less than US$1 per day (60p; Aus$1.60) does not earn enough to survive. In Europe, only around 3.5 per cent of the population (1.2 billion people) live on such a sum, but numbers are far higher in the **developing world**.

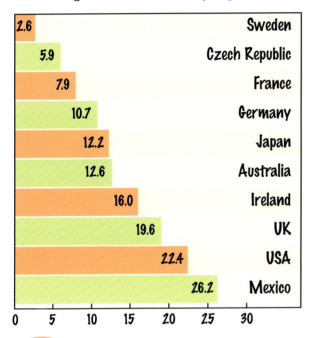

Country	Value
Sweden	2.6
Czech Republic	5.9
France	7.9
Germany	10.7
Japan	12.2
Australia	12.6
Ireland	16.0
UK	19.6
USA	22.4
Mexico	26.2

Graph from the World Bank showing per cent of children living below national poverty lines.

In rich countries, poverty is thought of in 'relative' terms – households receiving less than half of the national average income. The 'relatively poor' are excluded from the normal life enjoyed by others. Poverty re-emerged in rich countries in the 1980s, as unemployment and inequality rose.

A divided Britain

In Britain, politicians talk of 'two nations', and the 'north-south divide'. As the country grew richer, poverty increased. New wealth was concentrated in the hands of a few. Government figures in 1998 revealed one in four people (14 million) – 4.6 million of them children under 18 – lived in poverty, compared to fewer than one in ten adults and one in ten children in 1979. In 1999, Britain's top fifth of earners took 45 per cent of disposable income (the cash people have to spend). By contrast, only 6 per cent went to the poorest fifth of earners – down from 7 per cent in 1995–96, and 10 per cent in 1978.

Australia

Inequality also increased in Australia. In 1998, the poverty rate was the second highest in the developed world after the USA. Of particular concern were the numbers of homeless people and Aborigines (**indigenous** Australians) classed as poor at subsistence level (having only the bare necessities to survive).

UNICEF FACTS

In June 2000, UNICEF released figures showing the number of children living in poverty in developed nations.

UNICEF found that:
- *A child's chance of living in poverty is, on average, four times greater in single-parent families.*
- *There is a close relationship between child poverty and the percentage of households with children in which there is no adult in work.*
- *There is a close relationship between child poverty and the number of full-time workers who earn less than two-thirds of the national median wage.*
- *The countries with the lowest child poverty rates have the highest social spending.*

Inequality, poverty and migration

The greatest inequalities exist in the **developing world**, where the numbers living in poverty are staggering. According to the Catholic Fund for Overseas Development (CAFOD), of the 4.4 billion people in developing countries:

- three-fifths lack basic **sanitation**
- one-third have no access to clean water
- a quarter lack adequate housing
- a fifth have no access to health services
- a fifth of children do not finish primary school because they cannot afford to
- a fifth do not have adequate protein and energy from their food supplies.

In April 2000, **World Bank** figures showed that half the world's population survives on less than US$2 (£1.20/Aus$3.20) a day. They showed that a sixth of the earth's population – mostly in North America, Europe and Japan – receives 80 per cent of world income, an average of $70 a day.

Child labour

The International Labour Organization estimates that 120 million children aged 5–14 work full-time and a further 130 million part-time mainly in Asia, Africa and Latin America. Most children work because of poverty and raise about 20–25 per cent of family income. Some children are forced to work in the sex trade.

Poverty and migration

For hundreds of years, migrant workers – called 'swallows' – followed the harvests

Many businesses exploit child labour in the developing world.

around Europe, like migrating birds. Today, **refugees** flee political or religious persecution and war. The last 50 years have seen an exodus of people from their homes. According to the UN High Commissioner for Refugees (UNHCR) 25 million people have been forced from their countries. Another 25 million have been internally displaced, remaining in their country but forced from their land.

There has been negative publicity about modern refugees and **asylum-seekers**. This is not new. In 1900, Jews were expelled from Russia and the *Daily Mail* newspaper referred to 'so-called refugees' at Southampton. 'There were Russian Jews, Polish Jews…all kinds of Jews…they hid their gold and fawned and whined and…asked for money.'

Where the grass is greener

Global images of life in countries such as Britain and the United States will always tempt migrants who want a better life for their families. In Britain, life expectancy is 77 years and **infant mortality** 6 deaths per 1000 births. It must be attractive to people from countries wracked by civil war. In Sierra Leone, for example, life expectancy is only 37 years and infant mortality is 182 deaths per 1000 births.

Poverty has spurred migration for centuries, driving the Irish to Britain, colonists to Australia and New Zealand, and migrants to America, Brazil and Argentina. Even today, Mexicans smuggle themselves across the Rio Grande to work as cheap labour in the US. But borders have now closed – the world's poor are not wanted. Mass-migration can no longer ease the pressure of poverty and population growth.

Refugees arriving at a resettlement camp. Millions of refugees around the world are condemned to live in 'temporary' refugee camps – often for many years.

Poverty and indigenous peoples

News that Christopher Columbus 'discovered' America came as a surprise to the millions already there. When settlers arrived in Australia in 1788, there were one million Aborigines. By 1933, numbers had fallen to 66,000, due to disease and conflict. Numbers now stand at 250,000. New Zealand Maoris suffered a similar fate.

Health and inequality

Over the last 150 years public health measures in Britain have eradicated diseases such as cholera and diphtheria. In 1900, life expectancy was 48 years for women and 44 for men; today it is 80 and 75 respectively. **Infant mortality** has plummeted from 1 in 10 to 6 in 1000.

The health gap

As early as the 19th century, **reformers** noticed higher mortality and morbidity rates amongst the poor. Even today, poor people are more likely to be ill and die younger. A child born to a poor family in Britain will live, on average, seven years less than a child born to professional parents. And it is not just years of life – the child of the poor family has a greater chance of having their life soured by long-term sickness, disability, mental illness and insecurity. The UK government calls this 'the health gap'.

- Lower occupational groups experience more illness.
- Home-owners have less illness than people who rent their homes.
- Unemployed people suffer more illness than the employed.
- There is a health gap between northern industrial areas and rich southern areas.
- The health gap is *widening*.

> ## FACT
>
> - *The mortality rate is the number of deaths per thousand of the population per year. The morbidity rate is the rate of illness and disease.*

For many poor people, poverty and ill-health go hand in hand.

Cancer, coronary heart disease and stroke, mental illness and accidents kill three-quarters of those who die before the age of 75.

Cancer

- Unskilled workers are twice as likely to die from cancer as professionals.
- Women in north-east England have a 33 per cent greater than average chance of developing cervical cancer.
- Rich areas have better cancer survival rates than poor.

Smoking causes a third of cancer deaths; a fifth of all cancers are of the lung. Smoking is declining, but most slowly among unskilled people. Forty per cent of unskilled men smoke, but only 12 per cent of professional men do. Diet accounts for a quarter of cancer deaths. Diets low in fruit and vegetables are linked to several cancers. Evidence suggests healthy foods can be more expensive and so an inadequate diet is normal for many families. Some bacterial infections common in poor areas are linked to stomach cancer. Several cancers are linked to industrial chemicals, affecting people who work with them or live near contaminated sites.

Coronary heart disease and stroke

Coronary heart disease (CHD) is common in the developed world. It causes damage to the heart, leading to heart attacks. Strokes are caused when an artery is blocked or ruptured, cutting off blood to the brain. CHD causes 200,000 deaths in the UK every year:

- CHD deaths in people under 65 are three times higher in Manchester than the wealthy towns of Kingston and Richmond.
- CHD kills three times more unskilled men than professionals. This gap has widened over the last 20 years.

Smoking, poor nutrition, obesity (being overweight), lack of exercise and high blood pressure increase the risk of CHD. Obesity is high among manual workers and highest among the unskilled. Some poor people's diets contain too much fat and salt, and too little fruit and vegetables. People in unskilled occupations are more likely to be less active in leisure time.

Mental health

Poor people – particularly in inner cities – are at greatest risk of mental illness, such as depression. Suicide causes 4000 deaths annually. It is three times more common in men than women, and four times more likely among unskilled men than professionals.

- Unemployed people have double the risk of depression than the employed.
- Children in poor homes have three times more mental illness than those in wealthier homes.
- Homeless people are four times more likely to have mental illness than the general population.

Risks particularly affecting poor people include poor education, unemployment, social isolation, financial problems, crime, drug/alcohol misuse, injury in the womb or at birth.

ACTION

What can you do? You could find out what is being done to improve the situation, or discover who is responsible for making changes. Is illness inevitable? Or can people help themselves become healthier? And what about you? What is your attitude to health and illness? How do you feel about your own health and well-being?
Check out these websites:
Health Education Authority – www.hea.org.uk
The Children's Society – www.the-childrens-society.org.uk
You can also search the Government's official publications website for reports on a range of poverty, health and other related topics at www.official-documents.co.uk.

Personal health

and poverty

Some argue that because people *choose* to spend money on cigarettes and high-fat, high-salt foods, and *choose* not to exercise, it is their fault if they become ill.

Stubbing out cigarettes?

In 1999, the British government said, 'Smoking is the most powerful factor which determines whether people live beyond middle age.' Smoking contributes more than anything else to the 'health gap'. While many people smoke, numbers have declined, but the decline has been slowest among unskilled men and women. Why? Numbers starting to smoke are similar across social classes. But half of the better-off stop by their 30s, while three-quarters of those in the lowest income group carry on. Smoking rates are highest among people who are unemployed. They are especially high among single parents – research has shown that almost three-quarters of the poorest lone mothers smoke. One-third of all smokers in Britain are now concentrated in the poorest 10 per cent of earners. There are many reasons. Though nicotine is highly addictive and very dangerous, it can also offer short-term relief for anxiety, stress, depression, irritability, hunger – all factors particularly affecting poor people.

Many of us do not realize the harm our actions can have on others.

But do poor people simply behave in a way that harms their health more than better-off people? There are a number of things to consider:

- Even after factors like smoking have been taken into account, poor people suffer worse health than the effects of smoking and poor diet indicate.
- Advertising and the media make legal drugs such as cigarettes and alcohol very alluring.
- **Peer pressure** is a vital part of every young person's development, but it also influences decisions you must make about taking both legal and illegal drugs.
- A lot of people cannot find support to stop bad habits or break addictions.
- The opportunity to exercise is often limited by such factors as heavy traffic and pollution in urban areas, poor or expensive facilities and lack of provision for cycling or walking.

Other health factors are outside a person's control. In 1998, in Lambeth, Southwark and Lewisham in London, three of Britain's poorest boroughs, it was found that people with worse adult health were more likely to have:

- been a low birth weight baby. Babies who are small at birth because of poor nutrition in the womb risk heart disease, diabetes, stroke and high blood pressure in adult life
- suffered serious illness in childhood
- had an unskilled or semi-skilled father
- lived in a home lacking basic amenities
- had relatively poor growth in childhood
- had a poor education. People with higher educational qualifications usually have better health.

FACTS

Childhood poverty is linked to:
- *respiratory disease, diabetes, cancer, heart disease and stroke in adulthood*
- *increased disability in later life. This may be due to the increased injury risk in manual occupations*
- *an increased risk of unemployment from age 36*
- *increased risk of hospital admission and increased length of stay between the ages of 36 and 43.*

Tuberculosis

Throughout the developed world, infectious diseases associated with poverty have also made a comeback. Tuberculosis (TB) thrives in poor environments and among people already weakened by poverty or **malnutrition**. For example, the Russian chief of prisons announced that 100,000 Russian inmates have active TB.

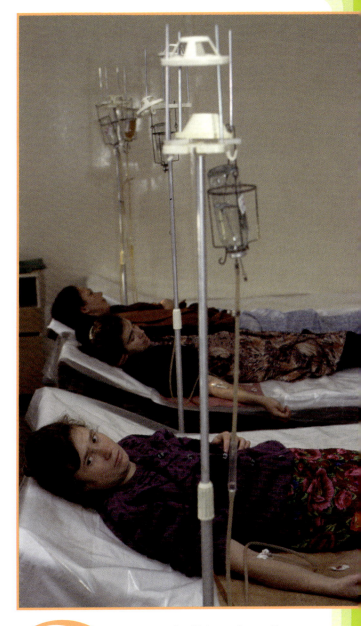

Patients being treated for Tuberculosis. Drug-resistant TB developed because many people could not afford to complete their treatment – the disease not only survived treatment but grew more powerful!

In a recent TB outbreak in the United States, several hundred people were treated in New York, one of the wealthiest cities in the world. The victims were people at the bottom of the social ladder, living in appalling conditions. Only prompt action by health workers prevented a more serious crisis.

Poverty, health and indigenous people

There are major differences in the health of the rich and poor in developed countries. This is even more striking if we look at the health of **indigenous** peoples kept out of the general increase in prosperity because of **discrimination** and **prejudice**.

By 1999, according to the Organization of Economic Cooperation and Development, the Australian **economy** had been growing continuously for nine straight years – the longest growth since the 1960s. There was employment growth, a reduction in unemployment, higher productivity – the amount produced by each person in employment – and low **inflation**. In 1999, Australian **Gross National Product (GNP)** per capita – for each person – stood at US$20,650. (Britain's stood at US$20,870.) It was a very rosy picture.

However, the Australian Bureau of Statistics reported that indigenous Australians were dying younger and in higher numbers than the rest of the Australian population. Their mortality rate was three times that of the whole Australian population. The largest differences were among people aged 35–54 years old, where death rates were 7 times higher. Fifty-three per cent of

indigenous Australian men and 41 per cent of women will die before the age of 50. By contrast, in the wider Australian population, 13 per cent of males and 7 per cent of females will die before they are 50.

Many indigenous Australians have found themselves excluded from the general increase in wealth.

16

Links to poverty

Like most developed nations, heart disease, stroke, injury, cancer, respiratory diseases and glandular illnesses account for three-quarters of all deaths in Australia. But there were more deaths among indigenous males and females for virtually every cause:

- three times more deaths from heart disease and stroke among indigenous males; 20 times more deaths from rheumatic heart disease
- five times more deaths from respiratory diseases, and nine times more from pneumonia and influenza
- six times more deaths from glandular illnesses
- 40 per cent more deaths from cancer
- sixteen times more deaths from diabetes among females and nine times more among males.

These are all health problems that have proven links to poverty, parental poverty and **malnutrition**.

There were also many more deaths as a result of violence and accidents, drugs and alcohol – causes that have their greatest effect on poor people. For example, death rates from injury were three times greater, the death rate for murder and assault was seven to eight times higher, suicide and self-inflicted injury was 40 per cent more common among females and 70 per cent among males.

Infant mortality is also closely related to poverty. Sudden Infant Death Syndrome (SIDS) or cot death is six times more likely among indigenous males and seven times among females. Indigenous infant mortality rates are 70 per 1000 for males and 80 per 1000 for females, compared to a general Australian rate of 5 per 1000.

For many years, indigenous Australians did not benefit from the increase in wealth through the rest of Australia. The rates of premature death and ill health they now suffer are the continuing consequences of their poverty and social **exclusion**. It is not just in Australia: higher than average death rates have also been found amongst the indigenous natives of New Zealand, Brazil, Mexico and North America.

FACT

- *GNP per capita lets us compare the wealth of countries with small populations to that of more populous countries. GNP divided by the population gives the per capita – per person – wealth. To make comparisons even easier, it is shown in US dollars. If we compare Switzerland (population less than 7 million, GNP of US$286 billion in 1995) with the United States (population almost 249 million, GNP US$7100 billion), we see that in 1995, Switzerland had a GNP per capita of US$40,630, while the US only had a GNP per capita of US$26,980.*

ACTION

Want to know more? Check out the Australian Bureau of Statistics website for information on a range of social and economic topics – www.abs.gov.au. There are also many library books about the treatment of indigenous peoples.

Malnutrition and illness

Our idea of **malnutrition** is usually a child with stick-like limbs, a wrinkled sack of bones, eyes vacant in a face old before its time. Famines are dreadful, but despite the distressing image, they are unusual, normally made worse by conflict or natural disaster. However, malnutrition is usually a more gradual and subtle process – a cruel combination of poor diet and frequent illness. Poor nutrition in early life lowers resistance to disease, causes poor physical growth and interferes with brain development.

At the moment, children under five account for more than a quarter of global deaths. Almost all of these are in the **developing world**, where, according to UNICEF, malnutrition affects one-third of all under-fives. It does not have to be extreme. Of the 13 million under-fives who die every year, 7 million are malnourished. Of these, 5.6 million are only mildly or moderately malnourished. Beating malnutrition also means tackling diseases that thrive in bodies weakened by poor nutrition. Eighty-five per cent of deaths (10.6 million) are the result of infectious diseases, nearly half of them diarrhoeal diseases, such as cholera. Lives can be saved relatively cheaply – through vaccination, **oral re-hydration therapy (ORT)**, provision of clean water and basic education. However, many developing countries find themselves in difficult financial situations and unable to afford these life-saving measures.

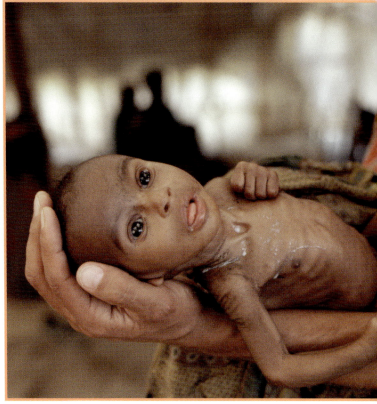

Shocking though this image might be, headline-grabbing famines actually kill far fewer people than slow malnutrition.

> **FACT**
>
> ● *Malnutrition affects the health of the next generation even before it is born. A pregnant mother's diet has a huge impact on the child she carries. Babies weighing less than 2.5 kilograms at birth have 40 times the risk of dying soon after, and a 50 per cent greater risk of serious developmental problems, heart disease, diabetes and premature death in adulthood.*

According to UNICEF, over 20 million babies born each year – mostly in developing countries – weigh less than 2.5 kilograms. Causes include inadequate nutrition before and during pregnancy, teenage pregnancy, workload during pregnancy and smoking. Seventy per cent of underweight babies are born in South Asia and sub-Saharan Africa. Improving the nutrition of adolescent girls and pregnant women can go a long way in preventing this problem.

The effects of war

Major famines occurred in Ethiopia in the 1980s and in 2000, during times of war. The causes were environmental – no rain fell, crops failed, cattle died – but conflict made it more difficult for Ethiopia to help its own people. In Somalia in the 1990s, the government collapsed and the country split into rival chiefdoms. International relief agencies withdrew, disease ran wild and ordinary people starved. War also creates huge **refugee** crises that increase the risk of famine, malnutrition and disease.

Disease

Many serious, often fatal, diseases are preventable. For example, cholera is a water-borne infection that causes violent diarrhoea and can kill within 24 hours. Treatment normally involves re-hydrating the patient and replacing lost minerals. Cholera killed thousands in the cities of Victorian Britain but was eradicated by **sanitation** and other public health measures. Cholera recently returned to Latin America in **epidemic** proportions – in October 1993, 900,000 cases were detected and 8000 people died. Soon after, a new strain (type) emerged in

southern Asia causing a second epidemic. Diseases such as cholera, pneumonia, influenza ('flu), TB and measles have the greatest impact on people already weakened by poverty and malnutrition.

WHAT IS TO BE DONE?

Death rates from many diseases have fallen in the developing world, thanks to simple hygiene measures and education. However, many of the causes of disease are beyond the control of ordinary people. These include flood, drought and famine, war, economic change, population growth, migration, inadequate health provision and changes to ecosystems. There are also problems linked to the lack of trained personnel such as doctors, scientists and public health officials.

The issue is not how individuals can protect themselves but what large organizations – especially governments – can do. And whether they can afford to do anything at all. Developing countries lack **resources**, skills and money. Also, as you will see, the **HIV/AIDS** epidemic and debt repayment are now placing huge and growing burdens on the social structure and **economies** of many developing countries.

ACTION

To find out more about disease and malnutrition in the developing world, visit these websites:
UNICEF – www.unicef.org
World Health Organization – www.who.int
Cafod – www.cafod.org.uk
Discovery Online – www.discovery.com

Poverty and the HIV/AIDS epidemic

Every minute, six young people are infected with the **AIDS** virus. Some 2.3 million people died of AIDS in 1997, and it is among the top ten killers worldwide. Africa suffers the most. Of 13 million AIDS deaths worldwide, 11 million have been in sub-Saharan Africa. 23 million Africans are infected – two-thirds of all cases. In Botswana, Namibia, Swaziland and Zimbabwe HIV is present in 20–26 per cent of 15-49-year-olds. In some parts, life expectancy has fallen by ten years.

Cause, consequence, cure

The **epidemic** has been caused by a lethal combination of factors – sexual behaviour, other sexually transmitted diseases, which leave people open to HIV infection,

poverty, **malnutrition** and poor diet, mother to baby transmission at birth, the high cost of treatment. According to the Joint United Nations Programme on HIV/AIDS (UNAIDS), health systems across Africa are devastated:

- nurses and doctors fall ill and die from AIDS
- HIV-infected patients occupy 50–80 per cent of hospital beds
- one year of basic medical costs for an AIDS patient is equivalent to two to three times a country's average yearly **GDP** per person.

Studies show that when AIDS strikes, agricultural production falls, threatening food supplies in town and country. The epidemic threatens to wipe out all the gains the **economy** has made in the last fifty years.

This map shows the impact of the AIDS/HIV epidemic throughout the world.

North America
900,000

Caribbean
360,000

Latin America
1.3 million

Western Europe
520,000

North Africa & Middle East
220,000

sub-Saharan Africa
24.5 million

Eastern Europe & Central Asia
420,000

East Asia & Pacific
530,000

South & South-East Asia
5.6 million

Australia & New Zealand
15,000

New drugs have cut death rates in the US and Western Europe. In May 2000, drugs companies announced a cut in treatment costs for developing nations, from US$16 dollars a day to US$2. However, 89 per cent of people with HIV/AIDS live in developing countries that account for less than 10 per cent of global **GNP**. With most of the population living on less than $2 a day, treatment is still expensive.

Effects on children

Because AIDS kills young adults, it leaves orphans. By 1998, a total of 8.2 million children had lost one or both parents to AIDS. For some of Africa's child soldiers, the **militias** are the only family they have known. While close relatives take some children in, urban growth, social disorder and migration are destroying family structures.

Prejudice and disgrace are still attached to AIDS. Because of these, many sick people do not visit clinics. In 1999, a South African AIDS campaigner, Gugu Dlamini, was beaten to death by a gang after announcing she was HIV-positive. 'Her death reminds us how stigmatizing AIDS still is, and how much courage it takes for people with HIV to be open about their condition,' UNAIDS Director, Peter Piot, said.

The developed world

HIV/AIDS is still a major problem in the developed world. Once ignorantly dismissed as a gay plague, it has rapidly become an illness of the poor. In the US, AIDS is the leading killer of young black men and the second leading killer of young black women. Prevention efforts in the US have not yet paid off – 75,000 people became infected in 1998, as many as the year before.

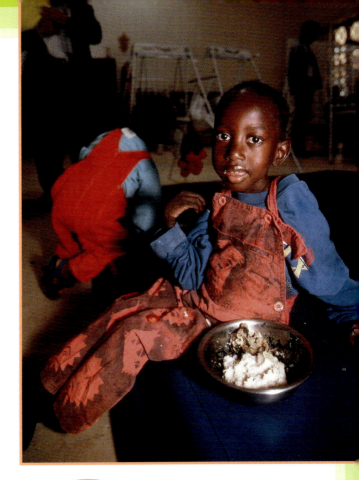

Children in an AIDS orphanage. Malnutrition and disease normally affects the young and the old: AIDS is wiping out the middle generation, leaving the elderly and the young to fend for themselves.

FACT

● *In Uganda, an education drive has encouraged Ugandans to delay the age of first sexual experience, take fewer partners and use condoms. New infections have dropped from 239,000 in 1987 to 57,000 in 1997. A workable HIV vaccine will also save lives. In 2000, the British Medical Research Council announced the start of human trials of a vaccine. Developments in understanding mother-to-child transmission also promise to reduce child infections where pregnant women can be tested.*

Housing in Britain

After food, shelter is crucial to survival. Britain's cities grew because industry needed workers and because **enclosure** of land drove people from the countryside. City life had rewards, but dirty and overcrowded conditions meant the poor fell victim to such diseases as cholera, typhoid, polio and diphtheria. For years, people campaigned to have neighbourhoods rebuilt.

Streets in the sky

As the first industrial nation, Britain was like a huge laboratory of everything that could go right and wrong during urbanization. The government soon realized that everyone benefited from proper sanitation and housing. By the middle of the 20th century, slums were replaced by tower blocks – 'streets in the sky'. But as old problems were solved, new ones emerged.

JACK THE RIPPER – HOUSING REFORMER?

Nineteenth-century Whitechapel, in London's East End, was a festering warren of slums. Demands for change were ignored. Finally, the outcry following Jack the Ripper's 'ghastly 'orrible murders' provoked action. The area was transformed with model dwellings, workshops, lighting and new **sanitation**.

Newer housing schemes have created as many problems as they solved.

Renting and buying

In 1979 in Britain, 32 per cent of all housing was rented from local councils. By 1996, it was only 18 per cent. The number of people living in their own homes rose from 55 to 67 per cent. The 1980s Right To Buy (RTB) policy encouraged people renting council houses to buy them. According to the organization Shelter, 216,130 council houses were sold under RTB in London alone. But local councils were prevented by central government from replacing houses. In north-east England, 2970 houses were sold, but only 10 were built. RTB left many local councils with the houses in which no one wanted to live.

In many areas today, especially London and the south-east, high house prices leave many people, even those in work and on good wages, unable to buy a home. Meanwhile, in poorer regions where there is little work, house prices are standing still or falling, so home-owners cannot afford to move to areas with jobs. In Britain as a whole, 14 per cent of all households live in poor housing – houses that are very damp, in disrepair or needing modernization. Poor people are most likely to live in bad housing. Most poor housing is in the large cities, and levels are twice as high in deprived areas. People in poor areas, living in poor housing, also suffer from social **exclusion**. The Government set up a Social Exclusion Unit (SEU) to tackle the problems they face.

In the country

Housing problems are not confined to the city. Wealthier people move to the country to find a better environment. They often commute to the city, adding to pollution and making the urban environment worse. Many people have a second home or a holiday cottage in the country. The process spoils the countryside. Villages are empty during the week, businesses decline, local people are unable to buy homes and, like poor people through the ages and throughout the world, they move to towns and cities to find accommodation.

FACT

Social exclusion describes what happens in areas with high unemployment, poor skills, low incomes, run-down housing, high crime rates, poor health and family breakdown. The Social Exclusion Unit (SEU) revealed that in Britain:
- *40 per cent of crime happens in only 10 per cent of the total area*
- *10 per cent of residents are burgled once or more a year, every year*
- *13 per cent of black people have been burgled – twice the figure for whites*
- *racial harassment and violence is widespread*
- *poor neighbourhoods face problems of anti-social behaviour caused by alcohol and drug abuse.*

In the 100 poorest areas, people are six times more likely to be unemployed. There is a shortage of skills and education. Robbery and attacks on staff force shops to close. Competition with supermarkets also forces small businesses to close. High crime pushes insurance beyond people's means, so they live without. Many fall prey to 'loan-sharks' who lend money at high rates of interest. Public facilities, such as schools and libraries, face bills for vandalism. This is money that would be better spent on new facilities and housing.

Housing in the developing world

In Britain, rich and poor often share streets and villages. In some countries, however, the rich are separated from the poor. In the USA, there are communities of African-Americans, Jewish-Americans, Cuban-Americans. Even among the rich the ghetto thrives, barricaded in walled estates against the outside world.

All round the globe, rich **elites** protect themselves from urban crime with barbed wire and security guards. In South Africa, architects design towns inside high-security compounds, with houses, shops, churches, leisure centres and even jogging trails. In Brazilian cities, walled highways link rich areas with the business centres. Many cut straight through poor **shantytowns** – the *favelas*.

Brazil

Brazil has one of the most unequal **economies** in the West. Ten per cent of the population take forty-seven per cent of the income, the poorest ten per cent earn less than one per cent. Education and other services are not government priorities. Less than one in five children of the poor completes primary school. According to the World Health Organization (WHO), life expectancy in Brazil is 63 years for men and 71 for women. UNICEF figures show **infant mortality** at 36 per 1000. Every year, 140,000 children die before their fifth birthday.

The favelas of Brazil. In their efforts to avoid travelling through them, many rich Brazilians now use helicopters – causing congestion in the skies above!

In Rio de Janeiro and São Paulo, the *favelas* sprawl across the hillsides, strongholds of drug gangs and poverty. In Rio they house one in five of the city's population. Visitors to São Paulo, the country's largest city, first notice luxury apartments, malls and skyscrapers.

24

Soweto was one of the 'townships' created by the apartheid government to keep black people and white people apart.

But built in the shadows of the buildings are shantytowns of cardboard, cinder block and corrugated tin. For most young people the choice is to join the gangs and risk an early grave or to suffer a lifetime of unemployment or menial labour. For a few, like the football player Romario, there is another way out.

In nations like Brazil, three or four generations might share accommodation in the *favela*. While a fortunate few might work in relatively well-paid jobs in factories owned by companies like Ford and Volkswagen, wages are still too low to support the whole family. Everyone who can must work. Child-care is entrusted to grandparents or great-grandparents.

South Africa

Johannesburg is the largest city in South Africa. It was founded after the discovery of gold in the Witswatersrand and is a centre of diamond processing, gold and commerce. Crime is a major problem with 300 street robberies a day. Rates of murder and assault are high. The city is ringed with shantytowns and townships built by the **apartheid** government for the black people who worked in the city. The most famous is Soweto (*South-West Township*). It was the scene of a major **uprising** against apartheid in 1976. Today it is still wracked by poverty and crime. **AIDS** fills Soweto's orphanages with sick, abandoned children.

Many settlements lack electricity, **sanitation**, education and health care. In Alexandria Township, six or more people sleep in cramped rooms of houses constructed from cinder blocks, old doors, tarpaulin, packing cases, even crushed coke cans. Like in Victorian England, extremes of wealth and poverty can be found next to each other in South Africa. You can see an executive barking into his mobile phone alongside a street-hawker selling statues made from wire; businessmen waiting for taxis where migrant workers sell single cigarettes.

Though ended, apartheid marked South Africa in many ways. Most whites live in secure suburbs, most blacks in townships. Most whites are rich, most blacks poor. However, South Africa still has as many as four million illegal immigrants. For many people, the search for a better life stumbled to a halt in the squatter camps. Not good, but better, perhaps, than Mozambique, Angola, Congo or Rwanda. South Africa has a male life expectancy of only 52 and a **GNP** per person of US$3210. But it compares well to Rwanda, for example, where male life expectancy is less than 40 and GNP per person is US$210.

The 'underclass'

In the 1990s, politicians and social scientists began to talk about an 'underclass' that was missing out on the general increase in prosperity. A vocabulary developed to describe them – 'long-term unemployed', 'chronically unemployable', and the ominous 'underwolves' that conjured up a picture of disorderly criminal predators. Different people were blamed for 'creating' the underclass – single parents, teenage mothers, absent fathers, fraudsters, teachers, minorities. Welfare benefits and the 1960s' sexual revolution were also blamed. Charles Murray, an American **sociologist**, claimed Britain was following the USA, where state welfare payments have created a dependency culture – a cycle of unemployment (and aversion to work), crime and single motherhood. 'A plague is spreading through our social fabric', he stated. In fact, single parenthood is usually caused by divorce. According to sociologist Joan Brown, the idea of marriage has been challenged throughout the whole of society.

Some people believe we have created an underclass on the run-down estates of our major cities.

The Thatcher era

Some people said the underclass was not new but consisted of people who had not adapted to the changes in the **economy** that took place in the 1980s. The election of Margaret Thatcher's Conservative government in Britain, in 1979, marked the beginning of major changes in the way governments managed their economies. The governments of developed countries abandoned their aim of employment for everyone and the idea that the countries needed heavy industry, manufacturing or mining to be strong. Such work could be left to nations with cheap labour, such as South Korea, Mexico, Taiwan and China. Instead, employment would be left to market forces.

Cycle of deprivation

For years, Britain enjoyed full employment, the unemployed being mostly people between jobs. After 1979, however, large labour-intensive industries were allowed to close. Labour-intensive refers to industries that rely on many workers, such as factories and mines. This left many areas without work. Unemployment rose sharply, beginning a cycle of deprivation – the end of full employment caused unskilled workers to fall off the bottom of the occupational ladder and become the underclass.

Major industries – coal-mining, steel, car-making, textiles, shipbuilding – declined or disappeared. Most of Britain's poorest areas are concentrated where these industries once were: the north-east and north-west of England; Scotland; Wales; the West Midlands; Yorkshire; Nottinghamshire; Merseyside.

Deregulation made the division of the country's wealth more unequal, says sociologist Gary Runcimon. It created a super-rich **elite** and a low-skilled, poorly educated service class (cleaners, fast-food workers, and so on). The creation of an underclass – the long-term unemployed – in many countries was part of this re-structuring. People who were unemployed because their skills were no longer wanted in turn created a generation without any skills at all.

The end of heavy industries like ship building in the 1980s meant a huge increase in the number of unemployed people where those industries had once been located.

The Bell Curve. Do our genes make us rich?

In 1994, **sociologists** Charles Murray and Richard Herrnstein published a book called *The Bell Curve: Intelligence and Class Structure in American Life*. The bell curve is a bell-shaped line on a graph showing income distribution in the USA. It starts low because of the relatively few people on low earnings, rises to show the number on middle incomes, then drops to illustrate the minority earning high incomes. Because a line measuring the distribution of **IQ** in the USA fits over the income line, Murray and Herrnstein claimed it proved a link between IQ and income, that the rich are also an intellectual **elite**.

Innate differences

The Bell Curve argues that poverty and the division of society into ranks are not caused by economic factors but **innate** differences in intelligence. Intelligence decides a person's education, businesses hire smart people, educated people get the best jobs. People with a low IQ fall behind. Because low IQ causes poverty and unemployment, government policies to alleviate them

actually create a dependency culture – a circle of unemployment, family breakdown, crime and reliance on state benefits. *The Bell Curve* argues that birth rates should be encouraged among intelligent families, and discouraged among those with a low IQ by ending measures to help them, such as state benefits.

The authors also claim that black people have lower IQs. Racism, they said, has little to do with inequality. When people of similar IQ are compared, blacks are

Hitler believed that the Germanic (Aryan) people were superior to any other and used eugenics to help keep the race pure.

more likely than whites to be doctors, lawyers, teachers and engineers. Differences in income and employment disappear, showing that inequality is due to IQ, not racism. They also argued that low-IQ immigrants threaten American society, and low-IQ migrants should be barred. Unless 'inferior people' stop having so many children, they argued, developed nations will become states where tyrannical **elites** rule urban reservations of the low-IQ underclass. Opponents of Herrnstein and Murray's ideas claim they are recommending a policy of eugenics (selective breeding).

FACT

● *At the end of the 19th century, the theory of eugenics was developed. It claimed that humankind could be improved by selective breeding. Since then, it has been used to justify policies based on class or race. Those who believed in eugenics blamed Britain's slow progress in the Boer War (1899–1902) on the 'degeneration [decline] of the Imperial Race'. Others realized that the frailty of British soldiers was a result of childhood poverty so free milk was introduced in schools. In the 1930s, Hitler used the eugenics theory to justify the **sterilization** and murder of disabled and mentally ill people, gypsies, Jews and the Slavs of the east. It was not just Nazi Germany. By 1943, 30 US states allowed sterilization of 'genetically unfit' individuals. Sweden had a policy of sterilization until the late 1960s. The former South African government followed a policy of 'separate development' (**apartheid** is Afrikaans for 'apartness').*

A flawed theory

Other social scientists have discovered that IQ scores in children have risen sharply over the past 50 years, and gaps in scores between all **ethnic** groups are closing. It has also been shown that Herrnstein and Murray chose statistics that fitted conveniently with their theories in *The Bell Curve*. IQ measurement has also been disputed since the early 20th century, because many supporters believed that intellectual development and social standing were fixed at birth.

The science is also not at all exact. In a reformatory (youth custody centre) in America, for example, every new inmate was tested from the 1930s on. In the 1940s, the average IQ jumped up, not because inmates became more intelligent, but because a different IQ test was introduced! For years in the Czech Republic, tests labelled gypsy children 'retarded'. But the tests did not accept cultural and language differences – most intelligent people would fail a test in a language they do not understand.

In the genes

However, the more we learn about **genes** and how they affect us, the more likely it seems that there *is* some genetic foundation to character, personality and intelligence. It seems equally unlikely, however, that they are solely the product of our genes. Learning from others as we grow up is a crucial part of making us who we are, and every one of us has opportunities we can make use of. As we will see, education is a very good example of these opportunities.

Education and opportunity

Even including winning the National Lottery, education is your best means of getting on in life! For every millionaire who dropped out of school, there are thousands who did not, and thousands of drop-outs who are not millionaires. The Institute of Education in London found academic achievement the single most important factor in later success. In the **developing world**, meanwhile, both **HIV/AIDS** and basic health care prove that education can mean the difference between life and death.

Whether a person can benefit from education or not often depends on wealth. In Britain, people from low-income households must overcome significant hurdles. In *A Class Act*, Andrew Adonis and Stephen Pollard describe Britain's school structure as 'educational **apartheid**' – the separation of social classes and systems. Wealthy people have a head start the world over, but separation is greater and starts sooner in Britain.

Private schools

Seven per cent of British children – ten per cent in London – are privately educated. They pay average annual fees of £6150 for day pupils and £10,500 for boarders. A *Financial Times* survey in 1999 revealed that 87 of the top 100 schools were in the private sector. Private schools are exam hothouses employing highly qualified teachers. Private schools boast facilities better than most universities. Teachers are better paid and parents and pupils deeply committed. The average pupil/teacher ratio is 1:10, compared to the state school average of 1:18. Almost 90 per cent of private school pupils go into further education and form 25 per

Many private schools boast facilities better than many universities!

CASE STUDY

In 2000, *The Guardian* newspaper compared Stanley Deason Comprehensive School on the poverty-stricken Whitehawk estate, Brighton, with the private Roedean Girls' School. The two schools are separated only by Roedean's grassy playing fields. Roedean's results are the best in the county. Before Stanley Deason was closed in 2000, only 10 per cent of its pupils gained five or more GCSE A–C grades. Many children had fallen behind by the time they got to the school – only one in ten year seven pupils had a reading age of eleven.

cent of university entrants. But private school pupils are not **innately** more intelligent, as studies have shown.

The picture is the same in primary schools. Private pupils are four years ahead of what is expected by age eleven. By contrast, in 1996, four out of five eleven-year-olds in one London borough failed a basic reading test. State schools consistently do less well than private ones. Eighty per cent of private school pupils pass five or more GCSEs at grade A–C. In state schools, only 43 per cent reach the same standard.

Truancy and failure

In deprived areas, pupils do much worse than average. Less than 15 per cent of pupils achieve five or more GCSEs at grade A–C. On poor estates, one in four children gains no GCSEs, and truancy is four times the average.

The National Child Development Survey showed a relationship between parents' earnings and children's performance. This is important because, as the Government confirms, deprivation has trebled since

Hackney Downs School in east London was closed by the government who believed it was failing to provide adequate teaching and motivation for its pupils.

1979 and a third of Britain's children – over four million – live in poverty. The British pupil failure rate is one of the highest in the **developed world**, but child poverty is also greater.

Differences in early development must also be considered. US research shows that educational prospects can be damaged before a child is three years old if they are not 'school ready'. Key factors affecting this include birth weight, early language development, mental well-being and reading by parents. At 22 months, children of parents in higher social classes have a 14 per cent higher educational development than those in the lowest.

Higher education

The majority of pupils entering Britain's best universities – especially Oxford and Cambridge (Oxbridge) – are from private schools. Entry is difficult but because it reflects well on schools, most admit coaching pupils applying to Oxbridge.

Governments have tried to open the system. By the 1960s, state school pupils made up 62 per cent of Oxbridge students, private school pupils 38 per cent. But by the 1990s, private school numbers had risen again to over 50 per cent.

Social bias

There is also bias towards higher social classes. In 1997–8, 80 per cent of Oxbridge first-year students came from

Many people believe that Britain's best-known higher educational institutions exclude many suitable candidates because of their social background.

the highest social classes while only eight per cent of all Oxbridge students were from the three lowest. In 2000, *The Times* reported that the chances of working-class children getting into a top university were less than one in a hundred and that half those admitted to Imperial College, the London School of Economics and University College, London, were privately educated.

This bias would not be so important if it were not for the influence of Oxbridge.

Of 250 people randomly selected from the 1996 *Who's Who*, Adonis and Pollard found 114 went to Oxbridge. Of the last nineteen Prime Ministers, Oxford provided nine and Cambridge three. Oxbridge graduates dominate the BBC's News Trainee scheme. 'In every walk of…life,' they conclude, 'Oxbridge dominates. A country of 57 million people is governed by 2 per cent of her graduate total.'

A divided system

Upper-class applicants are more likely to get into prestigious universities. Half the private school applicants with three A grades at A-level were accepted at Oxbridge, compared to under a third of state school applicants with the same grades. At the LSE, King's and University College applicants from 'posh' backgrounds are more successful, compared to students from poorer households.

Figures from the Higher Education Statistics Agency reveal a divided system. Oxbridge, Bristol, Edinburgh, Nottingham, St Andrews, Durham and Imperial College, London, take 70 per cent of their students from the highest social classes. In contrast, students from these backgrounds make up only 35 per cent at the New Universities – many former polytechnics – of Central Lancashire, Thames Valley, East London, Wolverhampton and Paisley.

Changes to student finance also hit poor families – student loans mean large debts. As a consequence, many decline to enter further education. For years, many people from poorer households entered higher education as mature students. However, in April 1999, the number dropped significantly. In one year, numbers fell by 7.6 per cent in the 21–24 age group, and 10.7 per cent for over–25s.

Though degree qualifications are supposed to be 'equal', degrees from the New Universities are not always as well regarded. For example, in the legal profession, statistics show Oxbridge graduates are six times more likely to get pupillage – traineeship with a law firm after completing a degree – than graduates from the New Universities. It is not because they are brighter. An Oxbridge graduate with a lower second class degree has a better chance of getting pupillage than a New University graduate with a first class degree. Medical schools have also been singled out for not taking students from poorer backgrounds.

Education in developing countries

Many people argue that education is neither luxury nor privilege, but a basic right. Of the world's poorest children 125 million are denied basic education. This number is equal to all children between six and fourteen in Europe and North America. **Illiteracy** keeps poor countries poor. In the **developing world**:

- one in four adults is illiterate
- women are 60 per cent more likely to be illiterate
- 150 million children who start school drop out
- in the 47 least developed countries, half the children do not go to school
- sixteen African countries saw school attendance drop in the 1990s
- in the 1980s, education spending fell by 65 per cent in Africa and 40 per cent in Latin America
- in parts of Egypt there are 12 girls to every 100 boys in school
- girls throughout the world fall behind, despite proven links between girls' education and the future health of families.

People without education are extremely poor, usually unhealthy, and die decades earlier than people with an education. They are open to terrible exploitation. For example, in Sierra Leone, Angola, Burma, Cambodia and many other countries, thousands of child soldiers are mentally or physically scarred. They are taking part in wars without reason, without end, without

Even where there are education opportunities for poorer children in the developing world, facilities are often meagre and classes overcrowded.

hope. In Asia, millions of girls become family skivvies or are sold as sex slaves.

Vicious cycle

Without education, a vicious cycle of ignorance, poverty and civil strife undermines nations. **Economies** crumble, countries collapse into chaos, **refugee** numbers increase. Estimates put the cost of primary education for all the world's children at US$8 billion annually. This is what the world spends on arms every four days and half what the USA spends on toys every year!

Education for all

Fifty years ago, the United Nations Declaration of Human Rights recognized education as a basic human right. In 1990, the world community promised primary education for all by 2000. In 1995, it was put back to 2015. Organizations have lobbied to make 2015 a real goal. Oxfam proposed a Global Plan of Action. In this, rich countries would provide US$4 billion a year through aid and debt relief, matched by developing countries diverting military and wasteful spending to education. Pakistan, for instance, spends six times more on the military than on primary education, while 11 million children are out of school and two in three adults are illiterate.

Many also believe the **World Bank** and **International Monetary Fund (IMF)** should change policies that demand the poor pay for education. Many cannot afford it and school enrolment rates have dropped in several countries as a result. Many governments, from Brazil to the Philippines, direct spending towards higher education that benefits the wealthy rather than towards basic education that benefits the poor.

LIFE IN SILICON–FAVELA!

In the 1990s, a computer expert opened up a computer school to teach new skills to the people of Brazil's *favelas* (shantytowns). By 2000, the Committee to Democratize Information Technology (CDI) had established 107 schools in *favelas* in 13 Brazilian states. In an interview, Rodrigo Baggio, nicknamed 'the Bill Gates of the Slums', said 'poor people in Brazil don't die of hunger, but because of a lack of opportunities'.

Schools run three-month courses to make young people computer-literate and give them useful skills. Teachers, from the *favelas* themselves, are trained by the CDI. Each earns £55 a month. The salary of nineteen-year-old Leandro, for example, makes up half his family's total income! Pupils tackle issues such as teenage pregnancy, violence and racism. They design posters and cards with social messages to teach skills and improve community awareness. 'What students want is better opportunities to earn money. That's easy. It's important to give them an understanding of social topics,' says Baggio.

The CDI has had such great success that it now works with other Latin American and African countries. Because of the respect CDI schools have in the *favelas*, no school has ever been broken into. But trouble exists outside – classrooms do not face the street to reduce risks of being hit by stray bullets! The CDI plans to put schools on the Internet, to create a digital community of *favelas*.

ACTION

Want to know more? Check out these websites:
Oxfam – www.oxfam.org.uk
United Nations Children's Fund – www.unicef.org
Christian Aid – www.christian-aid.org.uk
Save the Children Fund (UK) – www.scfuk.org.uk

The Great Depression

There have been times when poverty has been so overwhelming it has forced us to rethink all our ideas about it. The Great Depression of the 1930s was one such time. Its impact echoed around the world and it finally led to World War Two – a conflict costing almost 35 million lives. The Great Depression influenced the way governments ran their **economies** for many years after.

The Wall Street Crash

In the years after World War One, the United States became the world's most powerful nation. Between 1913 and 1929, its economy grew by 70 per cent. The New York Stock Exchange on Wall Street was the world's leading stock market. Companies raise money on a stock market by selling **shares** to **stockbrokers** and the public. These shares are then sold and bought, prices rising or falling depending on how each company is doing. Between 1927 and 1929, share prices on Wall Street rose spectacularly. This rapid rise persuaded people that prices would keep rising and that shares were a foolproof way of making money. People used their savings, borrowed from banks and even mortgaged homes to raise cash and buy more shares. Many bought shares by paying only a part of the cost, believing rising prices would allow them to pay debts and still make a profit. Many people owed huge sums. Then, on Thursday 24 October 1929, prices fell! Hoping to cash in before they lost everything, people tried to sell shares. But with everyone selling, prices fell faster and the market collapsed. Many shares were soon worthless! People owing to banks lost businesses and homes. Companies closed, throwing thousands out of work.

The effects of the Great Depression were so profound they challenged the imagination of almost every politician and policymaker around the world.

Panic!

The Wall Street Crash was not the start of the Great Depression, as it became known, but was its most dramatic episode. There had been signs for some time. Farmers had been hit by low prices and **recession** and many could not pay loans and mortgages. Banks began to cash in mortgages and confiscate farms. Many banks found themselves without cash. When customers tried to withdraw savings, banks locked their doors and refused to hand over money. This started a run on the banks – people panicked and besieged all the banks, even ones doing well. Some healthy banks were forced to close, causing even more panic!

Millions of Americans lost their jobs. Families lost homes and had to sell possessions. Without welfare, people relied on soup kitchens and homeless shelters, known as 'flophouses'. Farming families were forced from their lands in the Midwest. Many were drawn to California by the false promises of work and homes there.

Around the world

Because of the US economy's influence on the rest of the world, the Wall Street Crash made economic problems around the world much worse. Countries dependent on **exports** to the USA were hardest hit.

In Mexico, **imports** and exports fell by two-thirds and unemployment rose.

In Jarrow, north-east England, unemployment stood at 67.4 per cent in 1934. Hundreds of unemployed men marched almost 300 miles to London to publicise their plight.

It was made worse by the repatriation (enforced return) of Mexican workers from the US. In Australia, the depression increased unemployment and ended immigration. Development of industry and agriculture stopped, and agricultural exports fell.

In Britain, unemployment affected 2.9 million people. Areas that relied on exports – Scotland, the north of England and Wales – were worst hit. Only areas like south-east England remained relatively well-off. The fragile German economy was hit very hard. Unemployment was over 6 million by January 1932, from a working population of 20.5 million. In increasing numbers, desperate Germans looked to Adolf Hitler and the **Nazis** on the political extreme right, or to the revolutionary **Communists** and **Socialists** on the extreme left.

After the Depression

Until the Great Depression, **economists** believed unemployment was natural. As one source of employment declined, another developed, creating new jobs. Governments followed a *laissez faire* or 'leave alone' policy and did not interfere. But the scale of the crash was so bad something had to be done.

John Maynard Keynes

During the 1920s and 1930s, a British economist called John Maynard Keynes worked out his General Theory. It would become the foundation of economic policy in many countries until the 1970s. Normally, he said, people's spending helps to keep the economy healthy. In a depression, however, the unemployed have no money and people in work hang on to money because they are worried about the future. Keynes believed a government could increase confidence, economic growth and employment by creating jobs and stimulating demand. With increased demand comes more jobs, jobs increase people's confidence, and confidence increases spending. A government could pay for this by borrowing money. As the economy improves, increasing **taxes** can be used to repay the lenders.

In 1931 Keynes said, 'Whenever you save five shillings, you put a man out of work for a day.' He also explained that it was even better to employ a man to dig a hole then fill it in than to have him unemployed – because the worker then has wages to spend!

Trade barriers

Keynes was ignored in Britain, where governments cut spending. Because Britain had an **empire**, it was able to see off the worst effects of economic depression. It created trade barriers (special taxes) around the empire and made its colonies trade within it. Unemployment was still high, and stayed

A NEW IDEA?

Keynes' ideas were revolutionary – but not all were new. Some historians believe the Egyptian pyramids were built to keep farmers busy between harvests.

In the United States, the New Deal created thousands of jobs on huge construction and reclamation projects.

high, however. In 1941, two years after the outbreak of World War Two, there were still one million people unemployed in Britain!

Contrasting results

In 1932, Franklin D. Roosevelt was elected President of the USA. His 'New Deal' promised that the federal (central) government would use Keynesian-style measures to develop the economy. Projects included dam- and road-building programmes, environmental schemes, arts, agriculture and welfare programmes and laws controlling the minimum wage.

The contrast is interesting. In Britain, **Gross Domestic Product (GDP)** grew by 26 per cent between 1932 and 1939. In the same period, the GDP of the United States grew by 41 per cent.

The end of the Keynes era

From 1945 until 1979, almost all developed countries followed Keynesian policies to maintain full employment. However, many economists believed that full employment was difficult to keep up and caused **inflation**. From 1979,

countries all over the world abandoned Keynes. Tackling inflation became the priority instead of maintaining full employment. Many anti-inflation measures – such as raising interest rates and cutting government spending – increased unemployment and pushed down wages.

FACT

● *In Soviet Russia, there had been socialist rule since 1917. Socialism promised a society where individuals were free of the poverty and inequalities of capitalism. This meant ownership of industries and agriculture was taken away from individuals and put into the hands of the state. Shunned by their capitalist neighbours, Soviet governments looked inwards and were able to achieve rapid development of industry and infrastructure. During the first 'Five Year Plan' (1928–33), industrial output more than doubled. However, this was achieved at great cost. Millions of peasants died as a result of a policy of collectivization (state take-over) of farms, which led to famines.*

Margaret Thatcher's election victory in 1979 was the beginning of the end of Keynesian-style economic management throughout the developed world.

What causes poverty?

The gap between rich and poor countries is widening. In 1960, the world's wealthiest 20 per cent had 30 times the income of the poorest 20 per cent. By 1995, they had 82 times. Some African countries are poorer now than in 1960. Since 1970, income per person of average African households has fallen by 20 per cent. Many developing nations spend over one-third of revenues (annual income) on debt repayments. Basic needs – education, health, **infrastructure** – are unaffordable.

In 1984, while Ethiopians starved, the country was exporting food to repay its debt.

DEBT REPAYMENT

When a bank lends money, it charges interest. If £1000 is borrowed at 10 per cent annual interest, it means that £1000 (the principle) plus £100 interest must be paid back. If not paid within a year, interest builds up. Governments use interest rates to control economic activity. High interest makes borrowing expensive, so people delay buying houses, investing, and so on, and the **economy** slows down. Low interest makes borrowing cheap, so the economy speeds up.

Many countries borrowed billions of dollars at low interest rates from wealthy banks and other lenders in the West. The **World Bank** encouraged borrowing. 'There is no problem of developing countries being able to service [repay] debt,' it said in 1978. Then interest rates rose, trapping debtor nations. Unable to pay principle or interest, debts increased. Some nations, such as Ethiopia, exported food while suffering famine, to repay their debt.

For developing nations doing well, debt is a 'drag anchor' slowing economic and social development. Debt is carried by everyone, including the poor who often gain no benefit. To lessen economic problems and cut foreign debt, the Brazilian government sold off infrastructure, such as electricity companies and railways, to foreign companies – US$40 billion-worth in 1999 alone. The World Bank proposed wage and **pension** cuts and longer hours. Brazil could then borrow another US$42 billion to keep its economy afloat.

Money transferred abroad, often illegally, from countries made debt worse. At the same time as cutting wages and pensions for the poor, Brazil recently paid 40 per cent interest on savings to stop rich Brazilians sending money abroad.

In 1999, wealthy nations promised US$100 billion (£63 billion) for debt relief. But **International Monetary Fund (IMF)** figures show only moderate relief. Mozambique, for example, paying US$98 million a year in debt repayment would see this reduced to US$73 million. Despite debt, East Asia and Latin America have made progress. But several other factors trap many African nations in a cycle of poverty and war:

● Agricultural techniques have upset the environmental balance, with devastating consequences, for example, in Mozambique.

● **Empires** – British, French, German, Belgian – created many nations. Some are small and vulnerable, others contain a mix of **ethnic** rivalries.

● Independence left weak governments. Unstable countries were caught in vicious civil wars.

● **Apartheid** held back all of southern Africa.

● **Recessions** in developed nations hit **exports**.

● Economies have been badly managed. Many countries undertook expensive projects financed by loans.

● The IMF's 'cruel to be kind' strategy made cuts in health, education and **sanitation** a condition of debt relief.

Even healthy economies find themselves in difficulty. In 1997, the IMF and World Bank praised South Korea, Malaysia, Thailand, Indonesia and the Philippines as 'developing nations doing well by every measure'. Within months, all had collapsed into recession!

Even the fast-growing, so-called 'tiger economies' of the developing world, like Singapore, have been hit by recession and economic collapse.

The future?

What does the future hold where divisions between rich and poor are widening? In the **developed world**, wealth has become more concentrated. What will happen if people **monopolize** skills, education and new technology? And what will be the outcome for the underclass? As wealth becomes the only measure of a person's value in society, what will happen to the lower-paid professionals in health, education and public service?

What will be the consequences for the **developing world**? Will the monopolization of information and technology exclude them too? As rich nations claim **resources** for their own use, will future conflict be about resources – who gets them and how they are used? Meanwhile, poverty-stricken people look,

LAND REFORM

Around the world, people call for land reform. From Brazil to Zimbabwe, landless peasants occupy farms and stake out plots for themselves. These plots allow families to feed themselves, but do not produce a surplus that could be exported to bring in vital foreign currency.

with desperation, for answers to their plight. Some turn to religion, crime or revolution. Others take refuge in regional or **ethnic** identities. Some countries, like Sierra Leone, disintegrate into civil war. The chilling phrase '**ethnic cleansing**' enters the language.

'Natural' catastrophes, sometimes caused by pollution, intensive farming methods or deforestation, have their greatest impact on the poor. This is the aftermath of Hurricane Mitch in Honduras.

Environmental problems and climatic change are the consequences of industrial pollution, destruction of forests, the use of destructive farming methods. They in turn produce hurricanes, floods and droughts, which have their greatest impact on the poor.

Who can help?

Many organizations – religious, charitable and political – work to ease the effects of poverty, but admit in most cases they cannot match the scale of the problem. Realistically, only governments and international bodies like the **World Bank** and **IMF** can deal with debt, education and other problems.

Self-help

People do help themselves. In Brazil, the CDI brings computer education to the *favelas*. People start **cooperatives** to buy and distribute goods. On poor estates in Britain and the US, where banks have closed and loan sharks lend at huge interest rates, people create credit unions that make low-interest loans.

Losing ground

Developed nations can also become **underdeveloped**. Russia, for example, has 13 per cent of the world's oil, 36 per cent of its natural gas, huge coal and iron-ore reserves. But **Gross National Product** fell by half in ten years, industries closed, unemployment soared and the currency collapsed. Estimates put the number surviving by barter (swapping what they grow, make or find) at between a third and a half of the population – over 50 million people. In 1998, the British Medical Journal reported that average life expectancy in Russia fell by five years between 1990 and 1994.

> ## FACT
>
> *Sometimes poverty can provoke the poor into wrongly blaming others for their misfortune:*
> * *Across Europe discontented and **alienated** working-class youths join **neo-Nazi** movements to victimize immigrants and **refugees**.*
> * *In Russia, **anti-Semitic** groups attack Jews.*
> * *People talk of losing jobs to 'foreigners'. Dishonest politicians make use of such sentiments.*

Governments can reduce poverty. Nations around the world used the theories of John Maynard Keynes to maintain growth and employment. In Britain, in the 1940s, a civil servant called William Beveridge designed a welfare state to protect the people's health and well-being, which became the envy of the post-war world. The 'New Deal' in the US showed it was possible to act against unemployment and **depression**.

In the developing world, the priorities are health and education. Both offer the greatest chances for people to improve their lives. Even scant resources, used properly, can have a major impact.

What does the future hold if nothing is done? David Landes, in a book called *The Wealth and Poverty of Nations*, said, 'The rich countries' task, in our interest as well as theirs, is to help the poor become healthier and wealthier. If we do not, they will seek to take what they cannot make; and if they cannot earn by exporting commodities [goods], they will export people.' There are no empty territories open for migration and development. How we deal with the differences between rich and poor now will shape all our futures.

Glossary

alienated people who do not feel part of society and therefore feel nothing for its rules

anti-Semitic an opinion or action against Jewish people

Apartheid South African political system based on race that denied the black majority a vote and kept them out of positions of political and economic power

aristocracy nobles usually owing positions to inherited wealth or rank

asset thing owned that represents wealth, such as a house or a factory

asylum-seeker people seeking shelter from persecution

capitalism system that allows the private ownership of land, factories and so on by individuals

cooperative business owned by people grouping together for the common good

democratic a system where decisions are made, governments elected by a free and fair voting system

depression a slump in the economy

deregulation taking away government control of what firms can and cannot do

developed world countries that have gained wealth and influence through economic strength and development of industry

developing world countries that are trying to improve their economies. They are mostly agricultural, with low incomes and therefore low savings.

discrimination favouring one group over another because of race, sex, or religion

e-commerce using the Internet for business

economist person who studies how an economy works

economy the work done, the money earned, the wages spent, the goods produced in a single country

elite group of people at the top of society

empire countries ruled by another

enclosure fences put around open land in the 16th to the 18th centuries in Britain, which drove many people from the countryside and into the cities

epidemic outbreak of disease affecting many individuals

ethnic national, racial

ethnic cleansing expelling or killing people from geographical areas or countries because they are of the 'wrong' ethnic group

exclusion prevented from engaging in normal life enjoyed by others

gene inherited element of a living thing's make-up

Gross Domestic Product (GDP) the total money spent on goods and services in a country

Gross National Product (GNP) the total money spent on goods and services, plus income earned from investments abroad

HIV/AIDS Human Immunodeficiency Virus, and its later stage, Acquired Immunodeficiency Syndrome

illiteracy inability to read or write

import product brought into a country

indigenous a person born in a particular region

infant mortality number of children dying before their first birthday per thousand live births

inflation rising prices

infrastructure the elements of an economy that make the other parts work smoothly, for example railways, roads, power stations

innate inborn, inherited

International Monetary Fund (IMF) a branch of the United Nations, founded to promote international trade and monetary cooperation, and give financial aid to states

IQ (Intelligence Quotient) measure of intelligence

malnutrition lack of the essential nutrients and food needed to maintain complete health

militia irregular fighting unit or self-defence group, often under the command of a warlord

monopolize take complete control of the production and supply of an item

Nazi follower of Adolf Hitler and the National Socialist Party in Germany

neo-Nazi modern believer in the theories of Nazism and Adolf Hitler

oral re-hydration therapy (ORT) salt and sugar solution that prevents the dehydration associated with diarrhoeal diseases and raises the chances of full recovery

peer pressure going along with the crowd

pension money paid to a retired worker. Many people are encouraged to pay part of their wages while working into a pension fund.

prejudice preconceived ideas about people's attitudes, intelligence or abilities

recession minor economic depression

refugee person forced from their home by war or natural disaster

resources supply of money, labour, raw materials and so on that can be used by a country

sanitation clean water and improved sewage disposal

shantytown squatted area that has grown up in and around a major city of the developing world

share certificate issued by a company on a stock market to raise money

socialism the equal distribution of wealth between all and the common ownership of land, factories, banks and so on

sociologist person who studies society

sterilization surgery to prevent people having children

stockbroker person who buys and sells shares

tax money collected by government from wages and profits to fund such things as education, health and pensions

underdeveloped a country that has resources – land, labour, natural resources – that are not being used

uprising rebellion against the established order or authorities

World Bank the International Bank for Reconstruction and Development, established in 1945 to raise living standards in the developing world. Affiliated to the United Nations (UN).

Contacts and helplines

THE CATHOLIC FUND FOR OVERSEAS DEVELOPMENT (CAFOD)
Romero Close, Stockwell Road,
London SW9 9TY
020 7733 7900 – www.cafod.org.uk

CHILD POVERTY ACTION GROUP
94 White Lion Street, London N1 9PF
020 7837 7979 – www.cpag.org.uk

THE CHILDREN'S SOCIETY
Public Enquiry Point
The Children's Society, Edward Rudolf House,
Margery Street, London WC1X 0JL
020 7841 4436
www.the-childrens-society.org.uk

CHRISTIAN AID
35 Lower Marsh, Waterloo,
London SE1 7RT
020 7620 4444 – www.christian-aid.org.uk

THE JOSEPH ROWNTREE FOUNDATION
The Homestead, 40 Water End, York,
North Yorkshire YO30 6WP
01904 629241 – www.jrf.org.uk

JUBILEE 2000 (DEBT CAMPAIGN)
1 Rivington Street, London EC2A 3DT
020 7739 1000 – www.jubilee2000.com
(Also visit: Netaid – www.netaid.org)

OXFAM
Oxfam House, 274 Banbury Road,
Oxford OX2 7DZ
01865 313600 – www.oxfam.org.uk

SAVE THE CHILDREN FUND (UK)
17 Grove Lane, London SE5 8RD
020 7703 5400 – www.scfuk.org.uk

SHELTER: THE NATIONAL CAMPAIGN FOR HOMELESS PEOPLE
88 Old Street, London EC1V 9HU
020 7505 4699 – www.shelter.org.uk

GOVERNMENT INFORMATION SERVICES
Social Exclusion Unit –
www.cabinet-office.gov.uk/seu/
Department of the Environment, Transport and the Regions (DETR) – www.detr.gov.uk
Health Development Agency –
www.hda-online.org.uk
Our Healthier Nation – www.ohn.gov.uk
(Website produced by the HDA for the Department of Health)
LifeBytes: website giving young people aged 11–14 facts about health – www.lifebytes.gov.uk
Mindbodysoul: health website for young people aged 15–18 – www.mindbodysoul.gov.uk

UNITED NATIONS ORGANIZATIONS
United Nations Children's Fund (UNICEF)
www.unicef.org
United Nations High Commission for Refugees (UNHCR) – www.unhcr.ch
World Health Organization (WHO)
www.who.int
Joint United Nations Programme on HIV/AIDS (UNAIDS) – www.unaids.org
The World Bank – www.worldbank.org
The International Monetary Fund (IMF) –
www.imf.org

Newspapers

Many quality newspapers carry computerized databases of past articles – use their search engines to find out about poverty, debt crisis, health – for example:
The Guardian – www.guardianunlimited.co.uk
The Independent – www.independent.co.uk
The Daily Telegraph – www.telegraph.co.uk
BBC – news.bbc.co.uk
ITN – www.itn.co.uk

In Australia

Australian Charities – a very useful website directory of all the major charities – www.auscharity.org
Community Aid Abroad (Oxfam)
156 George Street, Fitzroy Victoria 3065, Australia
+61 (0)3 9289 9444 – www.caa.org.au

Labornet: information about trade unions in Australia – www.labor.org.au
The Australian – national newspaper website – www.news.com.au

Government Organizations

AusAID The Australian Overseas Aid Program
GPO Box 887, Canberra ACT 2601, Australia
+61 (0)2 6206 4000 – www.ausaid.gov.au
Health and Family Services (carries a range of links to other websites) – www.health.gov.au

Aboriginal and Torres Strait Islander Commission – www.atsic.gov.au
Australian Bureau of Statistics – www.abs.gov.au
Department of Immigration and Multicultural affairs – www.immi.gov.au
Commonwealth Dept of Family & Community Services
GPO Box 7788, Canberra Mail Centre
Canberra ACT 2610
www.facs.gov.au

Further reading

Fiction and personal memoirs

The Bed and Breakfast Star
Jacqueline Wilson, Nick Sharratt (Illustrator), Yearling Books

To Kill a Mockingbird
Harper Lee, Heinemann Educational

Brave New World
Aldous Huxley, Flamingo

Of Mice and Men
John Steinbeck, Elaine Steinbeck, Mandarin

The Grapes of Wrath
John Steinbeck, Mandarin

1984
Animal Farm
Down and Out in Paris and London
The Road to Wigan Pier
George Orwell, Penguin

Eva's Story
Evelyn Julia Kent, Eva Schloss, Castle Kent

Flo: Child Migrant from Liverpool
Flo Hickson, Anne Bott (Editor), Plowright Press

Non-fiction

The American West
Colin Shephard, Dave Martin, John Murray

Britain and the Slave Trade
Rosemary Rees, Heinemann Educational

Child Labour
Sandy Hobbs et al., ABC Clio

The Great Power Conflict After 1945
Peter Fisher, Stanley Thornes

The Holocaust
Reg Grant, Hodder Wayland

Mastering Modern World History
Norman Lowe, Macmillan Press Ltd

Modern Britain, Andrew Langley et al.
Heinemann Library

Native Peoples of North America
Susan Edmonds (Ed), Cambridge University Press

Profiles: Nelson Mandela
Sean Connolly, Heinemann Library

The New Deal: America 1932–45
J. Brooman, Longman

Riding the Rails: Teenagers on the Move During the Great Depression
Errol Lincoln Uys, TV Books Inc

Russia and the USSR: Pupil's Book
Terry Fiehn, John Murray

South Africa During the Years of Apartheid
Rob Sieborger et al., John Murray

Twentieth Century History
Tony McAleavy (Ed) et al., Cambridge University Press

Index

Titles in the *What's at issue* series include:

Hardback   0 431 03559 8

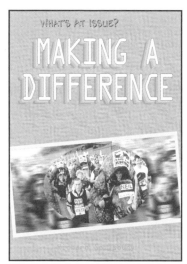

Hardback   0 431 03555 5

Hardback   0 431 03554 7

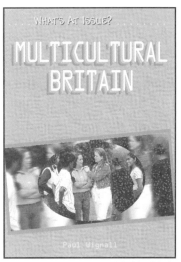

Hardback   0 431 03560 1

Hardback   0 431 03556 3

Hardback   0 431 03557 1

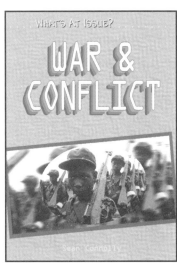

Hardback   0 431 03558 X

Find out about the other titles in this series on our website www.heinemann.co.uk/library